Speaking Out!

Insight Publishing
Sevierville, Tennessee

Published by Insight Publishing Company
P.O. Box 4189
Sevierville, Tennessee 37864

10 9 8 7 6 5 4 3 2

Printed in The United States

ISBN: 1-932863-57-5

Table Of Contents

A Message From The Publisher

Every day across America, and around the world, thousands of business professionals gather in conference rooms and convention centers for meetings—meetings meant to inspire, teach, or entertain. At each of these meetings, a professional speaker or trainer is retained, someone with proven expertise and a talent for delivering their message in a way that motivates people to take action, to change behavior, and to reach for success. These professionals have become a crucial component to business growth and the critical development of workers. In this edition of *Speaking Out*, we are proud to feature the proven strategies of seven of America's most dynamic and successful speakers. So, get out your highlighter and a legal pad—this book is loaded with information you'll want to begin applying to your business today!

David E. Wright, President

International Speakers Network

Chapter 1

Leadership, Integrity and Success

Nobby Lewandowski

♫ *"Start spreadin' the news, I'm leavin' today.*
I want to be a part of it, New York, New York."[1]

My presentations often begin by approaching the podium with a pink and yellow microphone that I've coerced from my six-year old granddaughter. I then begin singing along to a taped version of *New York, New York*. When I get to the second verse, I invite the audience to sing along.

I do this for one reason, and one reason only: Nearly everyone who stutters is able to sing with 100 percent fluency. We may sing off key but we're able to sing without stuttering; many people don't realize this. I do this to encourage people to listen to *what* I say and not the way I say it.

I do not want any sympathy because as a CPA I get paid by the hour.

---

[1] *Theme from New York, New York,* by John Kander and Fred Ebb

Warner Brothers Publications U.S. Inc., Miami, Florida, 33014

Introduction to the Author

Generally, I tell the audience a little about myself. I went to Benedictine High School, in Cleveland, Ohio, achieved success as a student and as an athlete. As a student, I was elected "Mr. Benedictine" which is the highest honor a senior can attain. I received many football scholarships, but had three concussions during my senior year of football; it was recommended to me that I not play any more football. I was offered a football scholarship from Kent State University. I thought it would be better for my health to ask, "How about a baseball scholarship?"

They asked what is a baseball scholarship, and I replied, "Well, it's the same thing as a football scholarship, but you don't get beaten up every day!"

I was very fortunate to receive the first baseball scholarship in the history of Kent State. If you're the first in anything, you have a major responsibility to everyone who follows.

Back in the 1950s universities weren't the same as they are now. I remember being a freshman and sitting in a large auditorium listening to the President of the University who said, "All men remain in the men's halls and all ladies remain in the ladies halls." I looked at my roommate next to me who became a little fidgety. The President added, "The first offense will be a $30 fine, second offense will be a $60 fine and the third offense will be a $100 fine." My roommate raised his hand and was acknowledged by the President. He asked, "How much is a season pass?" I knew right then and there I was in trouble. By some miracle, however, after majoring in baseball and minoring in accounting, I graduated.

I then signed a professional baseball contract and finished my career in the Pittsburgh Pirates organization. I have many fond memories of baseball; but in the 1960s baseball players were not making as much money as they're making now so I had to find a "real" job.

I went to work for the second largest CPA firm in the world. Then came April 6, 1965. The managing partner asked me to step into his office. He paid me nice compliments about my work on certified audits and said that my workpapers were very easy to follow.

I replied, "Thank you, sir."

He said, "We had you work on some complex individual income tax returns and we really like your analytical skills."

I again said, "Thank you, sir."

He then looked me in the eye and said, "This is very, very difficult, but I'm going to ask you to find a job somewhere in a back office where they can give you books and records, facts and figures, and where your inability to communicate will not have an adverse effect upon your business career."

With all the eloquence I could muster I said, "You've got to be kidding me (I didn't really say 'kidding,' but I'll have to use that word here)!" I thanked him for giving me the opportunity to work at the firm and said, "I have worked very hard and believe I have made good progress here." I continued, saying, "You are confusing the ability to speak fluently with the ability to communicate. There are people here I can listen to for fifteen minutes and still will not have understood what they've said."

So this hotshot husband had to go home and tell his wife he no longer had a job.

Back then my wife used to read several books a week. She handed me a book and told me to read it. The theme of the book was self-examination—what is your mission in life, what do you want to accomplish, what are your goals and objectives? So I read the book and I came back a week later with a listing of sixty-six different goals I was going to accomplish. They included objectives like owning a Mercedes automobile, becoming a millionaire, making a hole-in-one, making enough money for my children's education, meeting one new person every day, and as ridiculous as you may think this is, to one day become a nationally recognized motivational speaker.

After my wife read my completed list, she said, "How about finding a job?" which I thought was a very good idea, so I went out and found a job.

In 1970 I opened an accounting firm because I really believed there were people who wanted good accounting services offered by a sincere, honest, hard-working person who was able to care for their business as if it was his own. I built up the firm and it eventually became the eighteenth largest accounting firm in Northeastern Ohio with thirty-eight staff members. I inwardly perpetuated the firm and sold it when I was fifty-five. I am now enjoying life as an author, public speaker, business 'coach' and member of the board of directors for many companies.

I don't want accolades for becoming a speaker. I just hope that someone will come to the realization, "If *he* can do it, look what I might be able to accomplish!" Only in America can someone with a speech impediment become a paid public speaker. We all have a lot for which we should be thankful.

Playing the Hand You Are Dealt

Nothing I've done or said so far is as important as something I might say that will help you accomplish something good. I do not have *all* the answers and I'm not intending to preach. I just want to relate business experiences I've had and things I have learned and read. I'll share these with you in this chapter.

People often say to me, "Isn't it amazing that you have overcome your disability!" My reply is, "Isn't it nice that I have helped break down the superficial barriers created by society." I believe I've taken a liability and turned it into an asset; a handicap is only a handicap if you believe it is.

Having a speech impediment is not bad—when you make a one-hour speech you just have to prepare a fifty-minute outline.

I don't think of myself as a man who stutters, who was brought up in a lower-class household and who has made good. I think of myself as someone who, from an early age, knew he was responsible for himself and who had to make good.

My philosophy is that we live once on this earth and it's not a rehearsal, so whether you're big or small, fat or thin, tall or short, have a withered arm, are in a wheelchair or have a speech impediment, just make the best of what you have. Step outside of yourself; stop looking for sympathy from others and realize *you are responsible for your own destiny*. My philosophy has always been: if you are not living on the edge, you're taking up too much room.

What would have happened if I had waited to find fifty other people who stutter and then made an effort to make you understand us? You're busy with your own problems, so the faster I recognize I am responsible for my own destiny, the better my life will be. Playing the hand you're dealt—recognizing life isn't fair and many people have to struggle throughout life—the better off we'll all be. We have to put all obstacles and objections behind us and just get on with our lives.

Many people think "slow of speech, slow of mind." One percent of our population stutters, and four out of five stutterers are men (I'm not sure that women aren't the ones who make it happen, but nevertheless, it's a fact). On the average, stutterers, have a fourteen point higher I.Q. than non-stutterers.

When you believe something strong enough it doesn't matter what others believe. Just do it every day, be constant and consistent and you can make many good things happen. Maybe some of you have ulcers or are alcoholics. These problems are not as obvious as having a stutter—something that happens every time I speak—but I accept that I have it and I've tried to make the best of it.

Learn to see things as they really are, not as we imagine they are. How can you tell who a person really is? By watching what they do, not what they say.

My Thoughts About Leadership

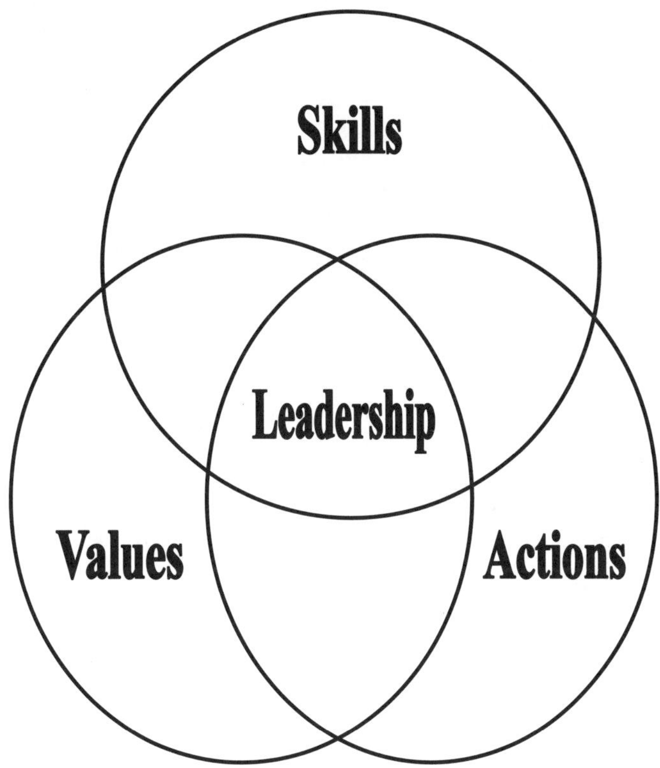

One of the greatest myths is that leaders are born and not made—the opposite is true. Leadership is earned, not granted. The following are some action items, skills and values that make the cream rise to the top.

Believing in yourself is very critical to becoming an effective leader. Many people have a low self-esteem—an inferiority complex. All my reading indicates that eighty-five percent of all people have a negative self-image. If you don't believe in yourself, you'll convey that belief to others. If you wait to change until it's easy or convenient, you'll never change. All change causes discomfort or uneasiness in some way.

I believe the greatest risk is not taking a risk. Learn from your mistakes and remember your successes.

I've learned that if you pursue happiness it will elude you, but if you focus on family, others' needs, work, meeting new people and doing the best you can, happiness will find you.

We're all going to have our peaks and valleys. We're going to have good days and bad days. I really like that story of a businessman who comes home from work, sees his wife and says, "What an awful day I had. I had to write off a $100,000 account receivable, I lost my biggest customer and my office manager walked out on me."

The wife looks at the husband and says, "Well, things haven't been real good around here either. Would you like to hear the good news or the bad news?"

The husband says, "I couldn't stand any more bad news. What is the good news?" She says, "The air bag worked." That puts things into perspective in a real big hurry.

Most leaders are just ordinary people who were thrust into a situation; performed well and liked it, and all of a sudden people began following them.

The true mark of a leader is willingness to stand alone and be counted. Leaders must have vision, good communication skills, tremendous empathy, compassion, and feeling. Management is of the mind, but leadership is of the heart.

Management is to checkers as leadership is to chess. To use a sports analogy: management is to football, as leadership is to basketball or hockey—more improvisation and unrehearsed results.

People will forget what you said.
People will forget what you did.
People will never forget how
you made them feel.
- Unknown

Real leaders have a high tolerance for mistakes, setbacks, and failures. They look at their co-workers recognizing that they have to occasionally fail. We can learn from our failures, and failures should never be criticized.

It's necessary to make people who work with us understand that decision-making is a critical part of advancement. They're not packing parachutes or doing open-heart surgery, so if they make a mistake it can be fixed.

Leaders have characteristics you can't hold in your hand—attributes like empathy, compassion, feeling, understanding, written and verbal communication skills and a high tolerance for errors. Ask any business owner and he will tell you, there's a significant lack of decision-making ability in the people he employs. Real leaders love to have people, they're bringing up through the ranks in an organization, who have the ability to make decisions. Whether it's right or wrong, these people make a decision and learn from their successes as well as mistakes.

We all tend to judge ourselves by our good intentions, but others judge us by our behavior. Maybe actions *do* speak louder than words.

What are you doing today to prepare yourself for where you want to be tomorrow, next year and in five years from now?

Without integrity you can never develop trust and without trust you can never develop people.

It would be wonderful if this whole world got back to the three R's:

- Respect for yourself,
- Respect for others,
- Respect for all our actions.

The very best short sentence I've ever heard has only ten words and each word has only two letters, "If it is to be, it is up to me." Life is like a boomerang, what you give you get back.

The cornerstones of success are character and integrity; and the words leaders should live by are responsibility and accountability. Wouldn't this be a wonderful world if our political leaders could look ahead and say, "I would like to have etched on my tombstone the saying, 'As I have watched you live your life as you believe, I have learned the meaning of integrity,'" which is another great saying I read somewhere.

If we really want to do something, we will find a way. If we don't really want to do something, we'll find an excuse. It is often easier to make an excuse than to face reality. Never do the easy wrong rather than the hard right.

The happiest people aren't those who have everything. The happiest people are those who make the best of everything. Are millionaires the happiest people? I don't think so. People may not have everything but they're thankful for what they have. If you walk around saying, "Boy, are things bad," one day you'll discover you're a prophet.

Elizabeth Plax says, "I would describe happiness as a certain level of inner peace and feeling of satisfaction with the family and friends that you have. If that's happiness, money is only going to add and subtract some, but it's not going to touch its core."

Leaders bring out the best in others and give the best of themselves. People will often follow the example they see every day from people they respect. I like the saying of the United States Air Force, "The difficult things we do immediately—the impossible takes a little longer."

If you look up the word "leadership" in the dictionary it will say, "the act of leading and thinking about the future." If you look up the word "leader" in the dictionary it will say, "A person who goes first and sets an example for others to follow."

Let's review many of the points I've made. Many of the characteristics seen in a leader are:

- Integrity
- Sincerity
- Positive Attitude
- Believe In Your Dream
- Work Hard
- Face Obstacles
- Vision—enlist others to help create your vision
- Confidence—necessary for every physical act
- Positive Self-Image
- Pick The Right Team
- People Management Skills
- Communication Skills (written and verbal)

If you are in business and want to be a successful leader, it is necessary to identify your weaknesses and pick the right people to make up for those weaknesses. I like to say, "managers do things right and leaders do the right things." Leaders have the guts to ask questions continually. Leaders have vision and a futuristic outlook that says here's where we're going.

We can all be very proud of what we've accomplished, but hopefully we realize that with hard work and extra dedication we can accomplish more.

How often have we heard the saying, "Before you criticize anyone, walk a mile in their shoes." What that really means is you'll be one mile away, have a brand new pair of shoes and they won't be able to hear you.

The four basic steps to becoming an effective leader are:

- Having a vision;
- Assessing strengths, weaknesses, opportunities and threats;
- Setting goals and objectives so they can be objectively measured;
- Providing motivation.

Leaders should realize that one of their main responsibilities is to motivate. Many effective leaders have learned the better they are to the people who work for them, the more money they make. It's as simple as that. If you're mean to your people—if you rant, rave and shout, you don't have empathy, compassion and sensitivity—they're not going to be highly motivated.

Effective leaders turn bold objectives, strategic financial and organizational goals into realities.

When you've gone so far that you think you can't manage one more step, then you've probably gone half the distance you're capable of. It's not how *many* ideas you have; it's how many ideas you *make happen* that counts.

The Seven C's of Leadership

Leadership is self-image. You can be appointed or you can be hired into a management position, but only your subordinates will judge if you are a leader. Hope is the main quality for change.

- **CONFIDENCE:** This comes from within. This is inner strength and how we can compensate for any deficiencies we may have so our subordinates perceive us as a confident person.
- **CONSISTENCY:** My father once said to me, "You can work for anyone as long as they're consistent." With consistency there is no place for double standards. Within an organization everyone has to be treated consistently.
- **CHARACTER:** This doesn't mean you should *be* one—it means you should have this characteristic. It means having high morals and high values. People should be able to say, "Yes, I trust you and am willing to follow you." I believe that character is doing the right thing when no one is looking.
- **COMPETENCE:** Competence is merely having the ability to do what you say you'll do. To quote an old baseball player, Dizzy Dean, "If you can do what you say you can do, that ain't braggin'."
- **COMMUNICATION:** How can you be an effective leader if you don't have written and verbal communication skills? You need to be able to "put all the pieces of the puzzle together" and explain your vision and how it needs to be fulfilled. To borrow a line from Stephen R. Covey's "*Seven Habits of Highly Successful People,* "You have to understand to be understood."
- **CHARISMA**: When I think of this word I immediately think of people like Martin Luther King, Jr., John F. Kennedy, Ronald Reagan and Lee Iacocca. A person doesn't have to be famous to have charisma. Maybe you can see this trait in your own family members, fellow employees, church members, and others.

In the mid 1950s Lee Iacocca brought a group of his engineers into a meeting and said he would like to bring back the convertible. He asked when he would be able to have a prototype. The consensus of opinion was that a prototype could probably be developed in seven to eight months. He replied, "What? All you have to do is take a chain saw, cut the roof off one of our existing automobiles and we'll have a convertible! Now, how is that for thinking outside the box? Then, to perform market research he drove the convertible around Detroit, Michigan, looking for reactions from people—either thumbs up or thumbs down.

I love acronyms. Here's a good one:

I – I
A – Am
C – Chairman
O – Of
C – Chrysler
C – Corporation
A – America

This man was born to be in that position with Chrysler.

Easter Sunday I was sitting in church and I thought of these acronyms:

L – Let's	L – Let's
E – Eliminate	E – Eliminate
N – Negative	N – Negative
T – Thinking	T – Thoughts

What a wonderful world this would be if we could get rid of negativism. My reading has revealed that ninety-five percent of the negative things we think about will never actually happen. Why waste all that energy on so many things that will never become a reality? Negativism is like sitting in a rocking chair—it gives you something to do but you don't get anywhere.

Another acronym to be an effective leader is:

T – Together
E – Each
A – Accomplish
M – More

Once a leader realizes that she or he is not an island and the thoughts, ideas, and energy of his or her teammates are needed to be effective, then more will be accomplished than ever could be accomplished individually. The leader conveys the vision, sets goals and objectives, assigns responsibilities, and then holds everyone accountable. Let everyone be involved in the decision making process. They'll accept ownership and they'll run through a brick wall for you if you give them ownership rather than merely a mandate about what has to be accomplished.

- **COMPASS:** A leader has to show direction. He has to show people a path to be followed that is time sensitive and follows all the natural laws.

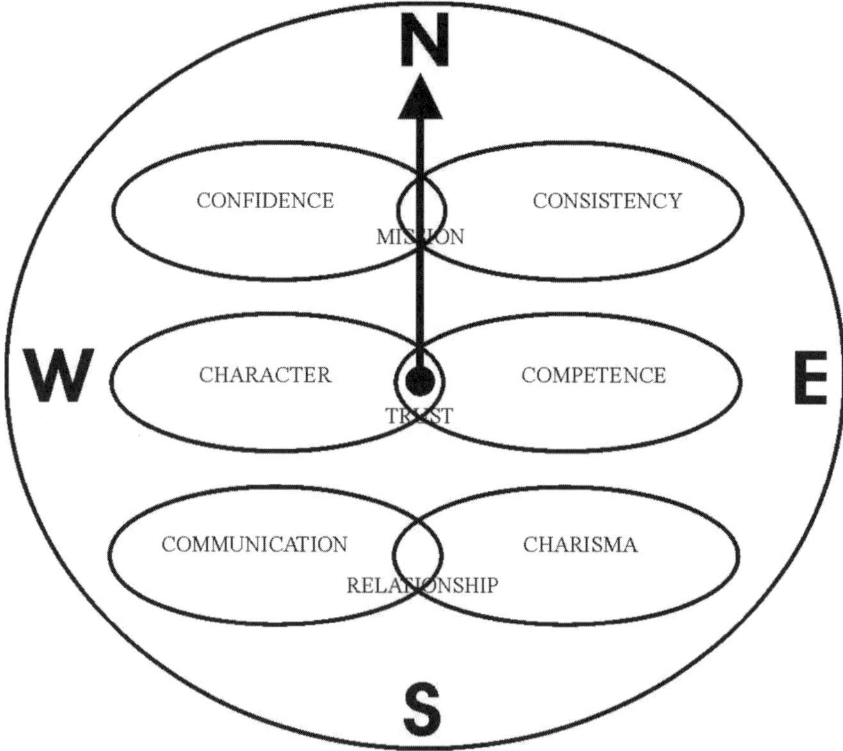

Here's a recap of the "Seven Cs of Leadership." If you exemplify confidence and consistency, it will demonstrate your mission. If you display character and competence, your subordinates will trust in you and do what has to be accomplished. Effective communication skills and charisma will aid you in forming mutually beneficial relationships. As you show direction with your compass, many good things can be accomplished.

Your Attitude Determines Your Altitude

The only thing that is constant is change.
Change is inevitable—growth is optional.

In the procedures manual of our CPA firm, our very first page read, "We Hire Great Attitudes." I believe attitude is everything. My study and experience has shown me that attitude is ten percent of what happens to you and ninety percent of how you react to what has happened. Probably not to your surprise, I have also developed an acronym for attitude:

A – All
T – The
T – Time
I – Integrity
T – Tenacity
U – Understanding
D – Determination
E – Enthusiasm

I once heard chocolate cookie businessman Wally "Famous" Amos say, "Age wrinkles the skin, but lack of enthusiasm wrinkles the soul." I love this saying and use it often.

Have you ever walked into work on a Monday and greeted a fellow employee asking how he was doing, and his reply was, "Not bad for a Monday"? Let him know that one-seventh of the rest of his life is going to be a Monday, so they'd better shape up!

Our lives are determined not by what happens to us but by how we react to what happens—not by what life brings us but by the attitude we bring to life. A positive attitude causes a chain reaction of positive thoughts, events, and results.

Everyone wants to win, but can you live with and learn from defeat and failure? I know from my own personal experience as a baseball pitcher that I learned more from a loss than I learned from a win because I was more analytical of the loss than the win.

People with a good attitude have enthusiasm and remain focused on their mission. Think about it: If you say, "Yes, I can accomplish that," or if you say, "No, I don't think I can accomplish that," you're absolutely right. How can you accomplish anything if you don't believe you're able to accomplish it? Whoever played a football or a baseball game and said, "I hope we don't win?" Everyone wants to win. You're never a loser unless you stop trying.

The most important things in life are invisible. These are the things that make us and mold us into what we are. What we see is passing; what we don't see lasts forever. Some examples are:

CHARACTER	ENTHUSIASM	LOVE
CONFIDENCE	HONESTY	LOYALTY
COURAGE	INTEGRITY	TRUTH

Things the eyes have never seen and your hands have never touched are the most important and enduring things in our lives. The good Lord never gives you more than you can handle; but sometimes you may think He has overestimated your abilities.

Effective leaders set goals for what they want to accomplish. All goal setting must be realistic, meaningful, and non-threatening. Goals need to be written; they must include specific deadlines, be organized, and they must be prioritized. Take one small step toward your goal every day. Remember, to measure success by this saying, "The yard is hard, but by the inch is a cinch."

SUCCESS

Ask yourself, "What single skill would have an extremely positive effect on my life if I did it very well?" If you practice that skill consistently it will elevate all your other skills. What a wonderful world this would be if we all did as well today as we expect to do tomorrow!

Success is the result of striving for perfection, hard work, learning from our failures, loyalty and persistence—success is where preparation and hard work meet.

Three Rules for Success

1. **Do What Is Right:** This is very simple—do what is right and avoid what is wrong. I'm not always sure what is right, but I can read the Bible or my daily local newspaper to get both sides of the story. It's not right to be dishonest, to cheat or to steal—there's no "twilight zone" for honesty. Things are either right or wrong. A good question to ask yourself is, "Would you act this way if your mother or your father or your

spouse were with you?" Ask yourself how this feels in your heart—if it doesn't feel right and you won't like yourself if you do it, you can bet it's wrong.

2. **Do The Best You Can:** Recognize that only one person can be the very best in anything. When you're an effective leader you don't use the same measuring stick for everyone—you ask everyone to give their best, recognizing that one person's best is not necessarily equal to someone else's best. Don't accept mediocrity. Keep things as simple as possible. When you put your head on the pillow at night you'll like yourself better if you know you've tried to do the best you could and know that you gave 100 percent of your effort.

3. **Treat Others as You Want to be Treated:** This is "The Golden Rule." Another version of this rule is what I term, "The Platinum Rule." The Platinum Rule emphasizes the need to treat others as they want to be treated and to recognize individual differences. No one cares how much you know until they know you care. This is the essence of teamwork—caring about your fellow workers. Additionally, recognizing the gender differences in communication can really help a leader succeed.

Three Universal Questions Everyone Asks

1. **Can I Trust You?** Do you mean what you say? Do you have integrity? Without trust there isn't a relationship between husband and wife, father and son, mother and daughter, employer and employee. Would a man have his automobile fixed by a mechanic that he didn't trust? Would he go there if the mechanic put in a new set of brakes and said they would work ninety-eight percent of the time? Would a woman go to a hairdresser if she didn't have complete trust? Would you go to a dentist who you don't trust? Trust is the essence of any relationship.

2. **Are You Committed To Excellence?** Do you really want to be great? Are you using everything within

your power to be the very best that you can be? I remember during the 1956 election, John F. Kennedy was asked if he wanted to run for vice-president. His answer was no. He explained that once you accept second place when first is in sight, you have a tendency to do that for the rest of your life. Are you really committed to the changing world we live in and accepting the fact that things are not easy and there is a price for any successes we may have?

3. **Do You Care About Me as a Person?** If we help someone else be successful, we'll find we also will be successful. One of the rules I instilled in any accounting firm and in many of the businesses and individuals my company represented was, "Under-promise and over-deliver; never over-promise and under-deliver." A successful leader is more helpful and shows more appreciation than his or her competition. We should all make a greater effort to show family, friends, and business associates how much they are appreciated and to say thank you.

This reminds me of a husband and wife going down a major interstate. The husband is going eighty-five miles an hour. He looks in his rearview mirror and says, "Uh-oh."

The police officer pulls him over and says, "Sir, I clocked you at eighty-five."

"But officer," the husband says, "I was doing sixty-five."

The officer replies, "I pointed my radar gun at you and you were doing eighty-five."

The husband said, "Officer, I set the speed control at sixty-five."

The wife says, "Harry, what are you arguing with the officer for? I heard you say, 'doggone it, I'm doing eighty-five—I think he has me.'"

The officer then says, "Look at you, you're not even buckled up!"

"Well, officer, I saw you walking up to my car, so I unbuckled to be able to reach my license."

The wife says, "Harry, I've heard you say, 'Why do they put these buckles in here? I'm never going to buckle up!'"

The officer looks into the car and says, "Pardon me, ma'am, is your husband always this argumentative?"

She says, "No, officer, only after he's been drinking!"

When I speak to various groups I like to make the next two points, which at first sound confusing, but are accurate:

- It's not what you *are* that holds you back, but what you *think* you are *not*.
- We are what we are because of what we think we are *not*.

Competition comes from within us; it's what's in our heart. Do we want to be the very best that we can be?

I can think of numerous examples. Reggie Miller makes approximately ninety-four percent of his foul shots; he practices fifty foul shots each night. Tiger Woods, Phil Michelson, and Ernie Els all make eighty percent of their six-foot putts. Why do you think they practice every day? Talk about adversity—think about Jackie Robinson, Willie Mays, Larry Doby. They were the first black baseball players in an all-white-man's sport. What about my former classmate, Lou Holtz—a 142-pound fourth-string linebacker on the Kent State University football team? Lou and I both remember being ridiculed by our peers who asked how we were ever going to make a living with our speech impediments. When Lou and I go to our speaking engagements these days, we often ask ourselves, where those people are now?

Think of all the people mentioned above—the sacrifices they made and how hard they worked to accomplish what they wanted. Now ask yourself where you want to be. Is it only wishful thinking or are you willing to pay the price and make the sacrifices necessary to accomplish what you really want to accomplish? A winner never stops trying. All limits are self-imposed, either by you or placed on you by someone with your implied permission. Don't let that happen.

A coach decided that Michael Jordan was not good enough to make his junior high basketball team in North Carolina and Michael was cut from the roster. That coach did not stop him from fulfilling a lifetime goal to be a great basketball player.

We all can accomplish more if we have perseverance. Life is full of these examples; go to school on them; learn from them. You will become a more effective contributor, and you'll like yourself better. There's talent and then there's achievement. Achievement is what you do with your talent.

During my speaking engagements, at the conclusion of presenting this material, I invite seven people from the audience to the stage and have them play instruments; again I bargained with my six-year-old granddaughter for these toys. They become my rock-and-roll band as the audience sings along to the 1960s hit by the Beach Boys, *Barbara Ann*:

♫ *Ah, ba ba ba, ba Barbara Ann, Ba ba ba ba Barbara Ann;*
Oh Barbara Ann, take my hand, Barbara Ann,
You got me rockin' and a-rollin', Rockin' and a-reelin'
Barbara Ann ba ba, Ba Barbara Ann. ♫[2]

Then I invite five people to the stage. I tell the audience about Hillary Clinton's book, *It Takes a Village and Other Lessons Children Teach Us*. "If this were a village, who would they be?" I ask. Somebody from the audience calls out, "The Village People!" I push the remote to begin the song Y.M.C.A, while handing the five performers Indian headgear, a construction worker's cap, a biker's cap, an Army hat and a policeman's cap.

♫ Young man, there's no need to feel down.
I said, young man, pick yourself off the ground. ♫[3]

After "YMCA" and after everyone has returned to their seats, I ask if there are any veterans, or parents, or brothers and sisters of those serving or have served in the United States Armed Forces in the audience. I hand each of them an American flag, and we honor these veterans by singing the *National Anthem*. Some tears are shed, but hopefully the audience has learned something about leadership while having a fun experience! Whatever the mind conceives, the body can accomplish—if the desire and willingness to get it done are there.

Work like you don't need the money.
Love like you've never been hurt.
Dance like nobody's watching.
Sing like nobody's listening.
Live life like it's heaven on earth.
-Unknown

---

[2] *Barbara Ann*
Words and Music by Fred Fassert
© 1959 (Renewed 1987) EMI LONGITUDE MUSIC and COUSINS MUSIC INC.
All Rights Controlled and Administered by EMI LONGITUDE MUSIC
All Rights Reserved International Copyright Secured, Used by Permission

[3] *YMCA*
© Can't Stop Music
Used By Permission
All Rights Reserved

About The Author

Nobby Lewandowski

Nobby had been active in sports since childhood and received combined athletic and academic scholarships to both Benedictine High School and Kent State University. He went on to pitch professional baseball, but at that time salaries were too low to support a growing family. Capitalizing on his bachelor of Science degree in Business Administration from Kent State University, Nobby obtained his Master from Case Western Reserve University where he majored in Banking and Finance with a minor in Taxation, and gained his CPA Certificate in 1964. In 1970, he co-founded and was Managing Partner of an accounting firm and ultimately led the firm to be among the "Top 25 Largest Accounting Firms in Northeastern, Ohio." At the age of 55, Nobby retired from the firm on July 1, 1992 and devotes his time to civic and charitable endeavors, along with involvement in outside business ventures and public speaking engagements. He serves on several corporate advisory boards and boards of directors. He has presented his seminars on Leadership, Integrity, and Success, on marketing professional services and accounting practice management to many professional groups. Offering a broad range of topics suitable for a variety of audiences and environments, Nobby is a truly gifted, and unconventional, public speaker who motivates and inspires in a highly entertaining format. From the moment he begins to speak, or maybe sing, he captures the attention of those in the audience and keeps them enthralled, energized and encourages. Nobby guarantees he'll leave audiences with much more to think about than when they arrived.

Nobby Lewandowski
3637 Medina Road, Suite 350
Medina, OH 44256
Phone: 330.723.1424
Fax: 330.722.7753
Email: nobby@apk.net

Chapter 2

Presentation Skills

Cynthia J. Small

Have you ever signed up for a conference or workshop but dreaded attending the session because of previous experiences that left you depressed rather than impressed? Do you remember listening to boring lectures after lunch that set the stage for an afternoon nap? And what about speakers who intended to take participants on flights of adventure but the journey ended up being more of a real trip to Never Ever Land? I must confess that as a participant, I have witnessed each of these situations and they were not pleasant experiences. On the flip side however, I have had opportunities to actively participate in trainings that left me energized, inspired and eager to return for more!

I must share one of the most exciting presentations I have ever witnessed which was a train-the-trainers conference in Florida a few years ago. I recall sitting on the edge of my seat from the beginning of the presentation to the very end totally amazed and pleasantly surprised. For me, the greatest aspect of this particular session was the creative way the presenter connected with the audience through a variety of innovative instructional methods. Not only did I gain valuable information from the content of the session, I also discovered powerful presentation tips that were creatively demonstrated and modeled by the presenter. This was indeed a participant-friendly session with lots of interaction and involvement in the learning process.

From this session alone, I have learned valuable instructional tools and techniques that may be applied in any setting with any audience.

For the past 10 years, I have had the opportunity to connect with diverse audiences and have discovered common threads for creating sessions that are meaningful, relevant, and participant-focused for optimal learning. I would like to share some of my personal experiences in making presentations to diverse audiences in a variety of settings. Additionally, I will introduce five "Checkpoints" for presenting a powerful message to any audience—students, parents, teachers, or various organizational teams. Many of the points and ideas that I will discuss are based on my experience as a classroom teacher, principal, youth director, college professor, and parent educator.

To present the five Checkpoints, I would like to set the stage by asking you to think about one of the best presentations you have ever experienced. Jot down some of the qualities of that particular presenter. Then take a moment to reflect on the impact this presentation had on your personal or professional life. Was it a meaningful opportunity that promoted positive results or growth in any way? Would you recommend this session to your colleagues? With these reflections in mind, I would like to take you on a special journey that is designed to empower and energize you with tools and the best practices for making powerful presentations. Please review the following five Checkpoints that will be discussed along the way:

1. *Make Reservations*
2. *Check Your Itinerary*
3. *Stand and Deliver First Class Presentations*
4. *Watch Out for Turbulence and Detours*
5. *Prepare for Landing*

Let the journey begin!

Checkpoint 1. Make Reservations—Plan With a Purpose in Mind

I am often asked to present workshops for parents in various school districts during the school year. Before I accept an engagement, I make sure to ask the purpose for the session and what's in it for the members of the audience. As a family life educator, I have made a commitment to conduct sessions that have a specific purpose and benefit to families, students, and the school. I am passionate about working with families and understand the important role parents play in the education of their children. Therefore, in order to present sessions that are meaningful and helpful to parents, I must have a plan in mind.

One of the first steps to planning a presentation is to assess the needs and interests of the audience and adapt the session accordingly. For instance, whenever I am asked to conduct a parenting class, I often ask the person who initiates the workshop request if he or she has conducted a needs assessment with the parents they serve. In most cases, many of them have not and will let me know that this is something they are required to do before the school year ends. One of my goals as a presenter is to make sure that I address the needs and concerns of each school community and that my sessions are tailored to meet those identified needs. The following is a list of sample questions I share with schools to assess parents' needs prior to the workshop:

- What is one major concern you have regarding your child's education?
- When you attend a parent workshop, would you be interested in role-play activities that relate to the topic?
- From a list of parenting topics, rank the top three that are most important to you.
- Would you be interested in receiving resource materials and information from community agencies that offer services to families?

These are only a few sample questions that may be used as an assessment tool for parent workshops. Once completed and returned to the school, this instrument becomes a planning tool that may be used to customize and prepare a quality session based on participants' needs and interests.

Just as an architect needs a blueprint for building a house or a pilot needs a compass to determine the direction of a flight, the presenter needs a plan for creating a meaningful learning opportunity for participants. To effectively meet the needs of your audience, develop an action plan that includes workshop goals, ground rules, handouts, group activities, visual aides, training props, and the evaluation method or tool to assess the effectiveness of the overall session. For me, it's important to have a written plan or outline that clearly depicts the key components of the presentation and the method of delivery to the targeted audience. This plan is what I call the "Presenter's Compass" because it gives direction and introduces pathways for taking the audience to their final destination. Planning is a critical process of any presentation and is the key to a successful journey. Remember, if a presentation is worth presenting, it's worth planning.

Checkpoint 2. Check Your Itinerary- Set the Stage for Learning

Now that you have planned your presentation, it's time to check your itinerary. Carefully consider strategies to set the stage for a safe learning environment that is conducive to positive experiences for the audience. Prior to beginning a training session, I often put myself in the participants' shoes and consider what I would expect as a member of the audience. Next I examine the following questions as a presenter:

- What is the purpose of the journey?
- Who are the passengers? Are they bringing any excess baggage with them?
- What is our destination and how long will it take us to get there?
- Are there any stops/breaks along the way?
- What are the group guidelines for a successful journey?
- How will I appeal to diverse learning styles and meet individual needs?
- Have I checked my personal baggage at the door?

Checking your itinerary for any presentation primarily involves creating an atmosphere for learning so that the audience will feel free to participate actively rather than passively. It's important to help the participants feel comfortable in the session by preparing an environment that welcomes audience participation, questions and answers, role playing, and group discussions. As a kindergarten teacher, I remember walking into my classroom and thinking that my job was to create a stimulating environment for young children that would enhance the teaching and learning process. I then assessed my classroom and did a gap analysis to determine what else needed to be done to accomplish this goal. Along those same lines, I have discovered that it is also important to create a stimulating environment for training sessions that will be interesting to any audience—young or old.

One thing I recall from a teacher in-service that I will always remember is: "Your room talks to everyone who walks in." This is why I spend a great deal of time preparing the learning environment for my audience. I want to send a message of welcome to your comfort zone rather than a welcome to the Twilight Zone. Essentially, the time you take checking your itinerary will help to set the stage for a successful journey packed with adventure, interaction and positive energy.

Speaking of energy, it is sometimes a challenge to energize audiences, especially adults. This becomes very important particularly if the goal of the workshop is to motivate, inspire and synergize participants. The best way to accomplish this goal is to recognize that adults, like school-age students, have different learning styles. There are visual, auditory and kinesthetic—hands-on—learners who have various backgrounds and experiences. This means that presenters have the challenging mission to create a variety of activities that will appeal to each of the adult learning styles.

Personally, I am a "VAK learner" which means I learn best through a combination of visual, auditory and kinesthetic learning experiences. I appreciate presenters who appeal to my VAK learning style by offering a variety of activities that will help me focus, understand and apply the learning content.

Likewise as a presenter, it is essential to create opportunities for audiences to engage in a variety of content-related activities that will stimulate visual, auditory and kinesthetic learning. Classroom teachers as well as workshop presenters may find the following list helpful in maximizing sessions for diverse audiences and learning styles.

- **Visual**
- Power Point slides
- Pictures
- Demonstrations
- Videotapes
- Handouts
- Posters/Charts
- Articles
- Training props (blocks, koosh balls, index cards, pipe cleaners, stress balls, etc.)

- **Auditory**
- Audio tapes
- Brainstorming activities
- Sharing personal stories
- Music/songs
- Readings (quotes, poems, books, etc.)
- Audio slide presentations

- **Kinesthetic**
- Icebreakers
- Team activities
- Role Play exercises
- Brain Teasers
- Puzzles
- Manipulatives/training toys

Now that we have discussed some tools to add to your presentation, let's talk about things to leave out of your personal baggage as you begin your journey. It's important for presenters to check their personal baggage at the door prior to each presentation. What am I saying here? This is just a reminder to remove any personal biases or stereotypes that may prevent an open and objective discussion with your audience. This will help to lighten your load and create a realistic focus on the content of your presentation.

Let me share an example to further clarify this point. Consider this scenario: I have been invited to speak at a school where there have been major problems and negative media attention regarding the administration and teaching staff. Of course, after hearing or reading the news, I have formed my own opinion and beliefs on the subject. However it is my role as a presenter to erase these preconceived thoughts and concentrate on delivering the workshop content without imposing my personal judgments and feelings. As a presenter, it is also my professional responsibility to model objectivity, respect, and professional ethics on the journey for continuous growth and success for all learners. In this way, I am checking my personal baggage to make sure that I stand before the audience with only the absolute essentials for a safe and productive journey.

Checkpoint 3. Stand and Deliver First Class Presentations

I remember the first time I had to present at a conference to an audience of 500 people. The closer it got to the time for me to present, the more nervous I became. Even though I knew many of the people in the audience, somehow the butterflies in my stomach created a fear factor in me. To counter this attack, I began to reflect on a quote I read during a workshop which was, in my opinion, quite appropriate for this occasion. It stated, "It's okay to have butterflies when standing before an audience. The key is to get them all moving in the same direction." This same principle applies to connecting with your audience from beginning to end and making sure that they are going in the same direction with you as the journey begins. Easier said than done—I agree!

It's always a challenge for me to open my presentations and to create a hook for my audience. My dilemma is deciding which opener will be the best fit for my audience. As I begin to plan my opening remarks, I try to think of a creative energizer or connector to break the ice. I consider not only who is in the audience but also the time of the session, the physical learning environment, climate, and other factors that may impact the presentation.

One important step I repeatedly consider is beginning on a positive note and sharing information that will be interesting, relevant, and appealing to adult learners. For example, I once spoke to a group of teachers about the importance of communicating with parents. I started the session with an interactive exercise called "Things that make you go hmmm." In preparing this opener, I put myself in the shoes of a teacher. This was just a matter of reflecting back to my teaching days in an elementary classroom. I asked the teachers to listen carefully to a set of questions and after each to respond by saying in unison "hmmm." The following are some of the questions I used for this opening exercise:

- Do I call parents to report their child's progress or do I only contact parents to share bad news about the student?
- During a parent/teacher conference, am I doing all of the talking or do I allow parents to ask questions?
- Do I attend PTA meetings to communicate and work with parents or to get comp time for the following Friday?

This exercise is a simple and interesting way to get participants focused on the content while setting the stage for learning. This part of the presentation is an important step to building rapport and trust with the audience. In this instance, it was my way of connecting with the teachers to lay the foundation for a fun and positive learning experience.

I can honestly say I do not have a magic formula for making effective, powerful presentations. However, there are some practices and strategies I have found to be excellent and very useful with adult audiences. Take a look at the following simple ideas for presenters who take time to plan *first class presentations for first class audiences*:

- **P**repare a creative opener for each session.

- Respect all learners and learning styles.
- Exceed the expectations of your audience.
- State the goals and purpose of the session.
- Engage the audience in your presentation.
- Notice body language and red flags.
- Talk with expression and leave a lasting impression.
- Energize participants with a variety of activities and ideas.
- Reflect on personal stories and experiences.

One other consideration for delivering effective presentations is to add elements of creativity that will enhance the transfer of learning, increase participation, and provide meaningful learning opportunities. The following list includes a creative idea that may be used in a train-the-trainer workshop which focuses on *Making Powerful Presentations:*

Six Steps to Presenting Up-Beat Presentations:

1. **Warm Up** your audience.
   Begin with an energizer to break the ice and create a comfort zone for participants.
2. **Speak Up** and make points clear. Introduce key points by giving examples and providing interactive group activities and demonstrations.
3. **Pick Up** the pace and keep the session moving. Structure sessions so that participants do not become bored with too much time spent on one discussion topic. Make smooth transitions from one area to another by using relevant connecting activities and ideas.
4. **Wake Up** and listen to the audience. Tune in to the audience's body language and exercise flexibility to make adjustments as needed.
5. **Open Up** and be yourself. It's important not to copy what you have seen someone else do in another presentation because it may not work the same way for you. Be creative and use original ideas that reflect you.
6. **Look Up** and acknowledge the audience. Avoid reading notes verbatim and dwelling on lecture material only. Provide an interactive environment by introducing a variety of activities to encourage active participation in the learning process.

As our journey continues, let's shift gears to discuss distractions that can negatively impact a presentation. Think for a moment about some of the worst-case scenarios of presenters who did not appeal to your individual learning style or needs because of something they did or didn't do in their presentation. Take a look at my personal top 10 list of things I find annoying and distracting in a presenter.

Let's compare notes!

1. Reading verbatim from handouts
2. Sharing too many personal stories and sick jokes
3. Talking down to the audience
4. Using little or no voice inflection
5. Chewing gum and smacking lips
6. Bird walking—not sticking to the subject
7. Standing in one place with very little movement (like a statue)
8. Repetition of words such as all right, okay, well, uh, etc.
9. Talking past the timeframe allotted for the session
10. Jingling change or noisy objects in one's pockets

It's not only important for presenters to concentrate on what they *say* but also on what they *do*. Remember that actions speak louder than words. One of the best ways to detect your own presentation distracters is to ask someone to observe or videotape your presentation. Then you can get a closer look at what the audience really sees. You can then begin to polish your presentation skills and make necessary changes that will promote more successful adventures in the future.

Checkpoint 4. Watch Out for Turbulence and Detours

Have you ever experienced some kind of car trouble during a road trip such as a flat tire, running out of gas, or having to take an alternate route due to construction? Similarly, I have encountered unexpected challenges during a presentation that have lead to a detour in the training session. However, through many years of training diverse audiences, I have discovered strategies for navigating through unexpected turbulence or difficult times.

I must admit that this is not always easy. As a rule of thumb, I usually try to think proactively about possible roadblocks or barriers that may surface during my presentation. It's really important for me to remind the audience to fasten their seat belts at the beginning of the seminar and caution them about possible challenges ahead. This is usually the time when I introduce the ground rules to set the stage for a safe journey. When and if challenges arise, my goal as a presenter is to maintain professionalism, exercise patience, and always have a Plan B.

When you work with different audiences you never know what could possibly happen or when it will happen. A few years ago, I presented a parenting workshop to a group of 50 parents at an elementary school on a Tuesday night. While the parents were attending my workshop in the auditorium, their children were attending structured activities in the school gym. I had opened my session with an icebreaker, set the stage for learning, and introduced the key points of the session. The audience was energized and I felt we had formed a positive rapport in a pretty safe learning environment. Just as I was about to conduct a demonstration, three very loud bells sounded and everyone froze in their seats. I too stopped my presentation because as a former campus administrator, I had become sensitive to bells and what they meant in a school setting. I quickly recalled that three long bells indicate a fire drill. That's right! A fire drill on a Tuesday night was happening right in the middle of my presentation! We all waited a moment with some anxiety to see if it really was a fire drill. Soon the principal came into the auditorium and announced that the fire alarm had been triggered and we had to evacuate the building. We all exited quickly and assembled on the sidewalk across the street while the firemen conducted an investigation of the campus.

Meanwhile, I watched the parents as they frantically searched for their children to make sure that they were safe. Then I began to wonder what would happen next. My initial thought was that after all of this commotion the parents would probably grab their children and head home. But when the principal announced it was a false alarm and that everything was okay, the parents began filing back into the building to continue the workshop. I had to think quickly as a presenter about how to reconnect with my audience and adapt the presentation for the little time remaining in the session. To my surprise, the audience was quite flexible which made my job a lot easier. One thing I recall doing is asking the parents to reflect on what had just happened and how this incident related to their parenting role in putting out "fires" at home. Many of the responses were quite interesting and gave parents a chance to examine their own parenting styles as we transitioned back into the discussion topic.

I shared this personal story to let you know that as a presenter it is absolutely essential to be flexible and willing to adapt presentations as needed. This ability does not happen overnight but comes with experience and practice. Recognize that things may happen beyond your control in a session no matter what the location is or who is in your audience. For example, you may encounter difficult questions that may be irrelevant or an interruption to your presentation. You may be unfortunate and have a know-it-all participant who is seeking attention or who just thinks that he/she is an expert on the topic being presented. What do you do?

I'll let you in on a little secret. Since I always strive to be a **STAR** presenter, I use these acronyms when responding to difficult questions, challenges, or interruptions in the learning process.

Stop, look, and listen to verbal and nonverbal signals.
Think before you speak.
Acknowledge the participant calmly.
Respect the ideas and feelings of others.

I admit that some sessions can be more challenging than others. When this happens, your first instinct may be to step out of your professional box and perhaps lose your cool. Maintaining your composure and respect for the audience is the first step in responding to any challenge. Even if you have showoffs or so-called "experts" who know everything about the workshop topic, it's critical to model a calm and positive attitude.

Please recognize that during your encounter with difficult participants, you have the right to remain silent, take a deep breath and say something like "that is an interesting thought. Thanks for sharing. Why don't we list this topic on our parking lot chart and address it in further details after the break?" Essentially, consider a method for redirection so that you can steer the audience back on course and continue your journey.

It's important to create a sense of teamwork in your sessions and to let participants know that we are all interdependent and can certainly learn from one another. This will help to create meaningful discussions and opportunities to exchange ideas. At the beginning of my sessions I often give this disclaimer: " I am not the expert on today's topic and I'm still under construction. I desire to learn from you as I share ideas from my personal and professional experiences."

As stated earlier, I also take time to introduce ground rules early on in my presentation that will set the stage for a safe, interactive learning environment. By sharing group guidelines at the beginning of a session, I am making an effort to promote respect, trust, and a positive rapport among the audience. Implementing this effective strategy with learners is a proactive way to prevent uncomfortable situations before they occur. Remember, it's better to be proactive than reactive!

Checkpoint 5. Prepare for Landing: Create Lasting Impressions

After presenting key discussion points and opportunities to apply the learning content, it's time to prepare for landing. What will you do to conclude your exciting adventure? How will you review what's been learned?

At this point in the presentation, consider capturing reflective thoughts in a creative and fun way. Please understand that you don't have to present a long, boring set of closing remarks to effectively end your session. In fact, I really feel this is the time to allow your creative juices to flow as you carefully orchestrate a way to remind participants of important key points and next steps for applying the information learned.

A creative closing activity can be accomplished through a variety of ways including the use of a relevant short story, poem, cartoon, quote, and even an audience sing-along session. Remember, this is your final opportunity to connect with your audience and to transfer the learning content in a meaningful way. To keep this in mind, use the following acronym as a reminder to add a creative closing to your journey. This slogan may be applied to any presentation and adapted for any audience:

Creatively
Leave an
Opportunity for a
Successful
Ending!

Using creativity, you can leave your autograph of excellence as you end on a high note with your audience. By taking time to plan creative closings, you can actually impact participants in a way that will increase their appetite with a hunger and thirst for continuous learning. Finally, as you provide an opportunity for attendees to reflect, you are allowing them to rewind and review the key stops that were made during the journey.

So, before your passengers reach their final destination, take a few minutes to prepare for a safe landing that will leave a lasting impression on your audience. Clear the runway and introduce creative closings and opportunities for reflections. By the way, when you allow time for reflections, this is a great reflection on you—the presenter!

Closing Thoughts

Each presentation you make—whether it is in a classroom or a boardroom, in a hotel ballroom or a school lunchroom—is an opportunity to take learners to a place that will strengthen their personal or professional lives. As the presenter, you can create the pathways to successful learning in any content area.

I hope that you will consider the five Checkpoints shared in this chapter as you prepare to take learners on meaningful and exciting adventures based on your area of expertise. Please keep in mind that these checkpoints may be adapted for all audiences and are essential components of a successful learning journey.

- Make Reservations—Plan With a Purpose
- Check Your Itinerary—Set the Stage for Learning
- Stand and Deliver First Class Presentations—Be the Best
- Watch Out for Turbulence and Detours—Have a Plan B
- Prepare for Landing—Create Lasting Impressions

As a presenter, I must admit that making a presentation—planned or impromptu—is not always an easy task. It does require practice, patience, and hard work to say the least. After each presentation, it's critical to review evaluations and feedback from your audience, assess areas for improvement, and build on personal strengths. By doing this, you will learn to grow from your experiences and escalate your presentations to the next level. As the navigator or captain of your adventure, you play a powerful role in turning ordinary presentations into extraordinary adventures in learning. Please remember that presentations don't have to be boring lectures and you hold the key to unlock fun and exciting learning opportunities for any audience.

As a presenter, remember to always check your personal baggage, have a Plan B, and polish your presentation skills continuously to create greater opportunities for teaching and learning. Don't forget your "presenter's compass" which will help to set the course or direction for an exciting journey that promotes personal, professional or spiritual enrichment. And finally, buckle up for the adventure of a lifetime as you soar with passion and energy in making powerful presentations that will make a difference in the lives of others. Have a safe and successful journey!

Presenter's Compass

Permission is granted to copy and use this planning tool to outline and organize your presentations and learning adventures. Feel free to adapt and personalize this checklist as needed to meet the needs of your audience. Let the journey begin!

Checkpoint 1. Make Reservations –Plan with a Purpose
Title of Presentation ______________________________Date_______
Time __________________Location____________________________
Event Theme _______________Audience________________________
Training Objectives____

____

Type of Presentation (lecture, workshop, keynote, etc.)__________

____

AV Needs __________________Room Setup____________________
Contact Person ________________Organization ________________
Phone _________________E-mail_______________________________

Checkpoint 2. Check Your Itinerary

- ✓ *How will I set the stage for learning? Where are we going and how will we get there safely?*
- ✓ *Ground Rules*

Checkpoint 3. Stand and Deliver First Class Presentations

- ✓ *Opening (icebreaker, group energizer, connecting with the audience)*
- ✓ *Key Discussion Points-*
- ✓ *Application -*

Checkpoint 4. Watch Out for Turbulence and Detours

- ✓ *Possible Detours -*

- ✓ *Plan B -*

Checkpoint 5. Prepare for Landing

- ✓ *Creative Closing – How will I review and reflect what has been discussed?*

Training Notes and Reminders

- ✓
- ✓
- ✓

About The Author

Cynthia J. Small

Cynthia J. Small is a Certified Family Life Educator who facilitates personal and professional development seminars for parents, educators and corporate teams. She has been an educator for more than 25 years and has served as a classroom teacher, campus administrator, and program director for parent involvement in the Dallas Independent School District. Presently, Cynthia is an adjunct faculty member in the Early Childhood Division at Brookhaven College in Dallas, Texas. As a trainer, Cynthia has developed several train-the-trainer modules to promote powerful presentations and workshops for diverse audiences. She has touched the lives of many individuals through her creative seminars, parent-teacher universities, and conference keynotes. Mrs. Small takes pride in not only developing workshops for adult learners but also *speaking out* to impact the lives of families and children throughout the world.

Cynthia J. Small
Family Dimensions
P. O. Box 112362
Carrollton, TX 75011-2362
Phone: 972-446-2608
Fax: 972-466-0691
Email: cajsmall@earthlink.net
www.familydimensionz.com

Chapter 3

Ten Strategies for Your Success

Joan Eleanor Gustafson

When I was fourteen years old, I had the opportunity to go to work one day with my Uncle Ralph, who had been my idol since I was a small child. During the drive to Ralph's office, I thought of the time that he was in the Marine Corps and had written wonderful letters back home. Since I wasn't old enough to read his letters at the time, he would take the time to interpret the letters for me by drawing some pictures. I was impressed with Uncle Ralph's letters and became even more impressed when he returned home. Having been the first person in our entire family to complete a college degree, he became a computer systems engineer.

My day at work with Uncle Ralph was during the time of the first generation of computers. This was during the time when a computer filled a room about the size of a gymnasium, when that same computer had a fraction of one percent of the power of the handheld computers of today. Nevertheless, I was fascinated by this technology and made a career decision that day to work with computers, following in Uncle Ralph's footsteps.

Although I had high goals and aspirations at age fourteen, I didn't do the things I needed to do in order to reach those goals. One of my high school graduation gifts was an engagement ring. Since I had been dating this boy for about five months and didn't want to hurt his feelings, I agreed to marry him. Shortly after we were married, I learned that my husband was deeply in debt. Because all of his income was needed to pay his past expenses, I had to work full time to support the two of us and could not afford to go to college. Knowing that most computer programming and systems analysis jobs required a college degree, I gave up on my goals.

The marriage ended in divorce. In my twenties, as the single mother and sole supporter of two children, I began worrying about my life, the choices I had made and my future. As I worried, I became physically ill with different types of ailments and spent most of my twenties in and out of hospitals.

Finally, when I was twenty-nine years old, my doctor said, "Joan, there's no way that you'll ever be able to work again. Your health will not sustain it. You need to quit your job, stay home and take care of yourself." So I quit work, stayed home and worried even more. My main worry was whether I'd even live long enough to see my two precious children grow up.

With more time available than ever before, I began reading whatever came into my home. It was then that I read a quote from William James that changed my life. He said, "The greatest discovery of my generation is that human beings can alter their lives by altering their attitudes of mind." After reading the quote several times, I realized that if I wanted to be successful in life, it was my decision. I had the power within me to control my life and my destiny. Not only would I alter my attitude, but I would also develop additional strategies for success.

After examining me a few months later, my doctor said, "I am amazed! I've never seen this happen before! You have recovered significantly and are well enough to go back to work part time." Integrating the strategies, I went back to school at night, earning both my bachelor's and my MBA degrees while working full time and raising my children. In succession, I became a computer programmer, systems analyst and systems supervisor. I later went into marketing and then into international management.

By using these success strategies, I became more and more successful in my international leadership career with the 3M corporation, which included a two-year assignment living in Paris, France, while maintaining offices in both France and Belgium. After retiring from 3M, my success continued into my professional speaking and consulting business.

In addition to being successful in my career, I'm fortunate to enjoy success in all facets of my life. Fourteen years ago, I met the love of my life, and we have been married for twelve years now. My husband,

Cliff, is the most understanding, supportive and compatible individual I could have ever dreamed of finding. I have two wonderful children, who are now adults. (I did live long enough to see them grow up.) My daughter has provided me with three of the most beautiful grandchildren you would ever want to see. I also have close relationships with my parents, my brothers and sister, and many friends. Reading that quote by William James started me on a path to success by choice, and I am extremely grateful that I found that quote so many years ago.

When I wrote my first book, I interviewed eighteen successful people. One of the first questions I asked them was how they defined success. Each person gave me a different definition of success, which helped to prove my theory that success comes from within each of us. Each of us can decide what success looks like to us, and we don't need to live up to anyone else's yardstick but our own.

I have been fortunate to share my success strategies with thousands of people throughout the years, and one of my joys in life is having the opportunity to witness the successful lives that these people have created for themselves. Although the following strategies are quite basic, I discovered that the integration of the strategies dramatically increases their results.

Success Strategy #1 - Believe in Yourself

This is the foundation strategy upon which the other strategies are built. Although most of my clients have high self-esteem, I've learned that even the most self-confident people have times when they don't feel quite as confident. These are usually the times when they are doing something new, when they need to stretch themselves outside of their comfort zones.

Each of us can develop the self-confidence needed to succeed. The following tips will help you to get started on this.

- Practice daily personal affirmations. In order to believe in yourself, you need to train your subconscious mind. Many of us have conditioned our subconscious mind in the past to believe that we are less than we are. The subconscious mind does not think for itself; therefore, it believes whatever is fed into it. If it hears negative comments, it believes them. If it hears positive comments, it believes them. Unfortunately, most of us hear, and pay attention to, many more negative comments than positive ones. That's why positive affirmations are so necessary. All of us need to train and retrain our subconscious mind by assuring that it is fed positive thoughts.

- Emulate self-confident people. Whom do you admire most? Does this person have some characteristics that you would like to emulate? If you decide to emulate some of this person's characteristics, you can be selective in the characteristics you choose. We can learn much just by observing people who appear to be self-confident.
- Reward yourself for each success. In a world where we have been raised to be modest and to not blow our own horns, it is often difficult to accept praise or even to admit that we are successful. However, recognition contributes to self-confidence, and we can't depend on others to give us this recognition. Genuine success comes from within. It is self-generated. It is the realization that we are accomplishing our goals and our missions in life. As we do this, we need to generate our own recognition. As we give recognition to ourselves for our accomplishments, we expand our enthusiasm and energy to accomplish more.
- Surround yourself with positive people. Olympic champion Wilma Rudolph was the twentieth of the twenty-two children in her family. Weak and frail as a child, she contracted pneumonia, scarlet fever and polio. As a result, her doctors had little hope that she would ever be able to walk. With the encouragement of her mother, Wilma worked at taking one step and then another until, at age eleven, she was able to make it from one side of her yard to the other. When she started high school, she made the basketball team and became one of the starting players when she was a senior. With much hard work, determination and more encouragement from her mother, she continued to improve her athletic abilities. At the Rome Olympic Games in 1960, she won three gold medals, set world records in both the 100-meter dash and the 200-meter dash and ran the anchor leg in the 4x100-meter relay. She was called the fastest woman on earth. When asked how she had overcome her disability, she responded, "The doctors said I would never walk. My mother said I would. I believed my mother."
- Not all of us have had the opportunity to live most of our lives with positive people, with people who encourage us, with people who do not criticize us. However, as adults, we can choose the people with whom we spend the majority of our time. As you include more positive people in your circle of friends, you will become more positive. As you become more positive, you will attract more posi-

tive people. As you attract more positive people into your life, your self-confidence will grow.

- Look and feel your best. Most people feel better about themselves when they look their best. We can do this by wearing clothes that are appropriate for the occasion, practicing good grooming habits, standing and sitting straight, getting enough sleep, maintaining good health, staying physically fit and wearing a smile.
- Fake it until you make it. Normally, I would not advise anyone to fake anything. Personal integrity is important to me, and I believe that honesty is critical to one's success. However, what I am recommending here is that you act the part of an extremely self-confident person. By acting self-confident, most people begin to realize that they can be self-confident. If people think of themselves as successful, they are successful.
- Affirm those around you. There are not many people in the world who can't benefit from more self-confidence. I have learned that even the most arrogant and seemingly self-assured people often lack the inner confidence needed to really feel good about themselves. Even these people need compliments. In business, the most confident executives and managers I know are the ones who give credit to their people who do the work. In life, the most confident people are the ones who demonstrate confidence in others.

The power of thought is so magnificent that it can change our lives. Through our thoughts, we are training our subconscious mind, which has been filled with garbage throughout our lives. Studies have been done with children to determine the number of positive comments and the number of negative comments they hear in a week. Depending on the study, the average number of positive comments ranges anywhere from forty to seventy, while the number of negative comments ranges anywhere from 500 to 800. These comments lodge themselves somewhere in the subconscious mind. By thinking positively about ourselves, we can fill our subconscious mind with the thoughts that will help us to be more successful.

Always remember that you are a special human being! Believe in yourself, and others will believe in you, also.

Success Strategy #2 - Dare to Dream

When I talk about dreaming, I'm talking about intentional dreaming, about actually taking the time from your day to relax, close your eyes and visualize what real success looks like to you. I had first heard about visualization about thirteen years ago when I was first dating my husband. We had gone to a lecture where the speaker was talking of visualization. As my husband-to-be was driving me home, I told him I thought visualization sounded "quite corny." I said, "I'm a successful person. I set my goals and achieve them, and I don't think I need this visualization stuff." It was then that my husband told me that he visualized frequently. Since I had much respect for him, I decided to try it.

Wishing to give the visualization process a big test, I set my first vision as one where I would sell my house and build my dream home. I had already purchased a lot on a beautiful pond, which was full of ducks and geese and had deer running around it. I had designed the house, but I couldn't start building it until I sold my current house. My house had been on the market for eight months, and I'd had no offers on it. My visualization was that, after an open house, the phone would ring, I would pick up the phone and hear the voice of my real estate agent saying, "Joan, a couple came through your house today, and they loved it! They made an offer, it's a full-price offer, and it's cash!" I thought, if I'm going to dream, I'm going to dream big! In my vision, the real estate agent added, "The buyers want to know if you can be ready to close and to move out in two weeks."

I visualized the sale of my home for two weeks before the open house. About three hours after the open house, my phone rang. The caller was the real estate agent, who said, "Joan, a couple came through your house today, and they loved it! They made an offer, and it's a full-price, cash offer!" He then added, "They want to know if you can be ready to close and move out in nine days!" I remember thinking to myself, "Wow, this visualization stuff is spooky!" My next thought was, "This is a fluke! It probably would have happened anyway." However, it aroused my interest enough to conduct more tests.

My new visualization tests included six new "creations," in different facets of my life—career, material possessions, relationships and spirituality. Each of these creations was as much of a stretch as selling my house. Within three months, all six of my creations materialized. As a result, I became a strong believer in the power of visualization!

As we train the subconscious mind through visualization, the subconscious mind helps to deliver the method for accomplishment. Since that first experience, I have used visualization as the first step in creating every major win in my life. I understand fully what Henry David Thoreau meant when he said, "If one advances confidently in the direction of his dreams, and endeavors to live the life which he has imagined, he will meet with success unexpected in common hours."

Visualization is not new. It has been used since the beginning of time. Aristotle said that the soul cannot think without pictures. "The reasoning mind thinks in the form of images… As the mind determines the objects it should pursue or avoid in terms of these images, even in the absence of sensation, it is stimulated to action when occupied with them."

The following process has created success for me in business and in life:

1. Determine what you want to create in your life.
2. Eliminate distractions.
3. Relax your body and your mind.
4. Create a mental movie.
5. Reinforce your vision through consistent mental rehearsal.

As human beings, not only can we dream, but we can make our dreams come true. Eleanor Roosevelt said, "The future belongs to those who believe in the beauty of their dreams."

May you always believe in the beauty of your dreams!

Success Strategy #3 - Determine Your Priorities

At one time, I thought I might have been one of the biggest victims of the superwoman syndrome. I was working full time, going to school at night and raising my two children by myself. I owned a house that I thought had to be spotless at all times. I was a perfectionist—so much so that I even scrubbed my kitchen floor on my hands and knees every night. I thought the reason I could get so much done was because I made lists. I still make lists because they help to get things out of my head and onto paper, allowing me to use my head for other things. My problem back then was that I didn't take time to prioritize my list. I'd just write action items as I thought of them and would then start at the top of the list and work my way down. Of course, the lists were always longer than the time available to accomplish all the items, so I'd transfer the unaccomplished tasks to my next list.

On one particular Friday evening, I made a weekend to-do list that was three pages long. Somewhere in the middle of page two, I wrote, "Call Grandma." At the time, my grandmother was seventy-eight years old. She was a dear woman. When I was sick during my twenties, she would call me every day to ask how I was feeling. When I was back at work, she'd call and say, "Joanie, I made spaghetti and meatballs today. Would you stop at my house after work and take this meal home for your dinner?" When I would arrive at Grandma's house, she would give me a box full of spaghetti, meatballs, lasagna and ravioli.

On this Friday evening, I was thinking of Grandma and decided to phone her over the weekend. I never got to this point on my list that weekend. Having a business meeting scheduled for Monday evening, I added "Call Grandma" to my Tuesday evening list. My grandmother died suddenly that Tuesday. I had not made that call, and, to this day, I still have dreams that Grandma comes back and says, "Joanie, it was a nightmare. I'm really here, and we can have that talk." But she's not here and never again will I have the opportunity to talk with my grandmother while on this earth.

Losing my grandmother in this way taught me an expensive lesson in priorities. I always said that my family was my priority, but I didn't live that way. As I was working on a time-consuming project, I would tell myself that as soon as the project was completed, I would take time for family, friends and myself. However, there was always another project waiting to be done, and I didn't live my stated priorities.

According to Stephen Covey, the things that we do can be classified two ways:

1. They're either important or not important.
2. They're either urgent or not urgent.

Most adults spend most of their time doing things that are urgent whether they are important or not. In order to live our priorities, we need to know our priorities. Knowing and living our priorities helps us to focus on the things that are important to us and to keep from becoming overwhelmed.

The following steps have worked for many successful people, and they will work for you:

1. Determine your true values.
2. Prioritize your value list.
3. Plan and prioritize your activities according to your value list.
4. Make time for your highest priorities.

This sounds simple, doesn't it? Amazingly, it really works! By using the methods specified above, we are able to make time to do those things that are most important to us. When our values are prioritized before writing a to-do list, we are better able to determine when an urgent item is an important item and act accordingly.

Success Strategy #4 - Set Powerful Goals

Although successful people are visionaries and intentional dreamers, they are also stable and goal-oriented. As Harvey Mackay said, "A goal is a dream with a deadline." Successful people have written goals. They communicate their goals, visualize the results and reward themselves and others for the accomplishment of milestones.

The following tips will help you to set and achieve powerful goals:

1. Before setting a goal, think about what you really want in your life. Many of us set goals to do what we think we should do; however, we may not want the results enough to remain committed to the goals.
2. Ask yourself if your goal is in alignment with your priorities in life. When a person's goal and priorities are not in alignment, a sense of being overwhelmed, or inertia, can stand in the way of accomplishing the goal.
3. Ensure that your goal is realistic and achievable. Many people give up on trying to reach their goals because they were hoping to achieve the impossible when they set those goals. However, it is also important to engage in possibility thinking and to realize that you are capable of achieving what others might consider impossible. Give your goal some "stretch."
4. Clearly state your goal by describing your desired results exactly as you wish them to be. State the goal in terms of what will be accomplished and when it will be accomplished.
5. Ensure that your goal is measurable by asking yourself how you will know whether you have achieved this goal.
6. Write your goal on paper, and keep this piece of paper in a place where you can look at it every day. Fewer than three percent of all adults have written goals, and research shows that people with written goals are more likely to achieve them.
7. Make a commitment to yourself to reach the goal, ensuring that you understand the effort that will be involved in doing this.
8. Visualize the end result. Close your eyes and create a mental movie of how the end result will look. In this mental movie, visualize yourself enjoying these re-

sults. Repeat this visualization daily, picturing yourself as if you have already achieved your goal.

9. Describe the benefits of your goal. Do this on paper so that you can read the benefits whenever you might struggle with doing the things needed to reach the goal.
10. Establish milestones as mini-goals, and write them down as well. It is easier to work on one small step at a time than on a big goal.
11. Develop and implement an action plan. Determine the steps that you will take in order to achieve your goal and write these down.
12. Communicate your goal to supportive people who might be able to contribute to its achievement, either through direct efforts or through encouragement.
13. Reward yourself as you reach milestones along the way to achieving your goal. By giving recognition to ourselves for our accomplishments, we expand our enthusiasm and energy to accomplish more.
14. Remain flexible. Although you will set a date for accomplishing your goal, there could be an emergency situation that you need to handle en route. When taking care of this situation is a higher priority than the goal, allow yourself to adjust your schedule for accomplishing the goal. Also, as you achieve your goals, you may change direction and will, of course, set new goals for yourself.
15. If you make a mistake, give yourself permission to start again. We are all in a constant process of growth and development. We can use our mistakes as learning opportunities and become even stronger than we had been previously.

Your goals, integrated with your dreams, will enhance your success, both in your business and in your personal life.

Success Strategy #5 - Take Action

Abraham Lincoln said, “Things may come to those who wait, but only the things left by those who hustle.” We build a foundation by visualizing what we want, determining our priorities and setting goals. Once this is done, it is necessary to move forward by taking action. In this rapidly changing world, standing still is like moving backwards. Action is a predecessor to success.

Often, the most difficult part of taking action is getting started. The best way to start is to first develop an action plan. Writing an action plan requires the action of writing. Your action plan can be simple or complex, depending on the nature of your goal. Once an action plan is in place, following this plan is as easy as following a recipe.

For writing your action plan, I recommend the following:

- List the steps in sequential order, even though some of them will be ongoing or overlapping during the process.
- Make sure that each step is measurable, i.e., you will know when the step has been completed.
- Visualize the end result.

Sigmund Freud once said, "Thought is action in rehearsal." I encourage you to rehearse your actions through thought, to develop action plans to achieve your major goals and then to follow your plans.

Now that we have covered the first five success strategies, it's important to know that these strategies gain a lot of power when they are integrated. If your beliefs, visions, priorities, goals and actions are synchronized, you will be able to create much more success in your life.

Strategy #6 - Stay Focused

Success requires concentration and focus on our vision, priorities and goals. However, ours is a time of shrinking concentration spans and less focus. Why are people focusing less now than before? I asked a cross-section of business people what they thought. Their answers ranged from the interruptions from all of the communications devices currently available to the multitasking mindset enabled by the television remote control.

Since we live in a fast-paced, hurry-up world, multitasking and getting things done fast are necessities of life. However, when we are working on a major goal, we need to set aside time just to focus on that goal.

Alexander Hamilton once said, "Men give me credit for genius. All the genius I have lies in this: When I have a subject in hand, I study it profoundly. Day and night, it is before me. I explore it in all its bearings. My mind becomes pervaded with it. Then... people are pleased to call [the effort that I made] the fruit of genius. It is the fruit of labor and thought." To this statement, I add that it is also the fruit of focus and concentration.

In today's complicated world, multiple distractions vie for our attention at any given time. The way we deal with these distractions determines how well we are able to focus on our goals and priorities. Following are some methods that successful people use to handle distractions:

- Set aside quiet time during the day to focus on your top priorities or action steps. During these quiet times, stay away from the telephone and other sources of interruption, allowing interruptions for emergencies only.
- Decrease the stress in your body and your mind by practicing relaxation exercises before you start focusing on a priority or action step.
- Keep a piece of paper and a pen at hand while you are concentrating on a project or task. When an unrelated thought enters your mind, write it down. These thoughts can be reviewed at a later time.
- Periodically, record your distractions and the methods you use to deal with them. Note the progress you are making in this area.

If we focus on winning, we will win. If we focus on accomplishing our goals, we will accomplish our goals. If we focus on success, we will be successful.

The key is to focus.

Success Strategy #7 - Remain Positive

With the things that are happening in today's world, it is sometimes difficult to maintain a positive outlook at all times. However, if we are positive, the people around us also become more positive. We are then able to become more successful and to help others to become successful.

At a 3M meeting several years ago, I met a woman named Mary, who was the champion of making lemonade when life dealt her lemons. I had never before known anyone with an attitude as positive as hers. At the beginning of the meeting, we all introduced ourselves and shared our reasons for our participation in this series of meetings. Mary had recently moved to St. Paul, Minnesota, from Washington, D.C. Her position in Washington had been eliminated. She told us that even though she had enjoyed her job there, losing it was a wonderful opportunity to look at other positions and to determine what she would like to do next. She found a position in Minnesota and rented an apartment about twenty-five miles from the office where she worked. She even talked about how fantastic it was to have an hour-long commute to and from her new job, as she was able to see much of the city and to listen to motivating tapes while she was driving.

Others who heard her told me later that they didn't think Mary was "for real." As I got to know her, though, I realized that she was truly genuine. As others in the group began to know her, they also realized it and strived to be more like her. They recognized that she was attracting positive people and things into her life through her attitude. Later, when I was hiring people for a new department, Mary was one of the first people I hired. Her attitude and enthusiasm were contagious, and she contributed significantly to the success of this department.

The following tips will help you to become more positive:

- As Dale Carnegie taught so many years ago, refrain from the three Cs: complaining, criticizing and condemning. They rob our time and also drag us down into a spiral of negativity. The messages they send to the subconscious mind inhibit our success. By eliminating complaining, criticizing and condemning, we become more positive. On the mental level, positive attracts positive, and negative attracts negative. Positive thoughts help to attract more positive experiences into our lives. This begins an upward spiral. As we begin to see things in a more positive way, we become more positive. As we become more positive, we increase our potential for success.

- Eliminate worry from your life. Just as most successful people do not waste time complaining, criticizing and condemning, they also do not waste time worrying. They realize that worry not only generates negative energy, but it also does not make the source of the worry any better.

  Shortly after I met my husband, Cliff, he had a heart attack. Afterward, I lived in constant fear that he would have another one. When I didn't hear from him at the beginning of a day, it would affect my thoughts on other things. Of course, Cliff sensed my anxiety, and this did not enhance our relationship. When I finally decided to stop worrying, our relationship blossomed, my mind became more clear for positive thoughts, I became more productive, people noticed my more positive attitude, and I was promoted at work. I learned that I could care, but that did not mean that I needed to worry.

  Many of us have serious concerns, such as life-threatening illnesses in our families. Worrying does not cure an illness, and we can become sick from the worry. Once we decide to stop worrying, we are better able to handle the situation that might have been the object of our worry.

- Put on a happy face. Have you ever noticed how people seem to want to please you more when you smile at them? To me, they appear to be more friendly and outgoing. When I realized this, I started to consciously observe people's reactions as I smiled at them while walking through the long corridors of 3M's office complex. I discovered that whenever I smiled, the recipient of the smile would return the smile. This, in turn, lifted my spirits. As a result, my smile became more genuine as I met the next person. As you smile at other people, you'll discover that your smiles are contagious.

- Look for the good in everything. I once attended a class given by a chiropractor who had developed an excellent chiropractic procedure, which not only included adjustments but also nutrition and forgiveness. During the class sessions, he discussed the subconscious mind and the fact that thought precedes action, even physical action/reaction within our bodies.

  This wise doctor of chiropractic explained that the secret to recovery in many of these cases was forgiveness. Sometimes, unknowingly, we carry grudges for things that happened to us at some time during our lives. If we do some serious soul-searching, we can determine if there might be people whom we have not forgiven. In class, we learned the three steps of forgiveness:

1. Forgive the person who may have wronged us.
2. Forgive ourselves for carrying the grudge, whether it was intentional or unintentional.
3. Look for the good in whatever it was that happened to us. This is the most difficult step, but it is necessary for the process to work.

There were some people in the class who were very ill and had traveled to doctors throughout the country in search of cures for their illnesses. It seemed to me that I saw miracles occurring that week when many of these ill people were relieved of their symptoms. In following up after the class, I learned that for most of these people, the symptoms never returned.

- Know that you can do it. A positive attitude, combined with self-affirmation, contributes to success. If you continually tell yourself that you can accomplish your objectives, you significantly increase the likelihood of doing just that. After being told that she could not be a stockbroker in her company because she was a woman, Dee Ray still knew that she could be a very good stockbroker. She changed companies and not only became an excellent stockbroker but later became a senior vice president and investment executive in her company.
- Laugh. There is healing power in laughter, and this power can heal us mentally and emotionally as well as physically. Laughter helps to release stress. After a long day at the office, a good laugh will revitalize me. It brings with it a good feeling, a feeling of lightness, a feeling of joy. I also find it enjoyable to spend time with people who have a sense of humor, as it is difficult to have both a good sense of humor and a bad attitude.
- Value other people. Each individual on this earth is a miracle. Each of us has unique skills, talents and abilities. We all live in a connected universe and contribute to the growth of one another. We are partners in the creation of good for all of us. As we show respect for others as individuals, we in turn gain respect.
- People are so precious, even those who seem to be cross and ornery and those who seem to stand in the way of our achieving our objectives. If we value them and show that we care about them as people, we might be surprised at the difference we will see in them.

By adjusting our attitude toward them, we might just see a change in their attitude toward us.

A positive attitude can open doors to opportunities. It has for Mary and for me, and it will for you, too!

Success Strategy #8 - Live Your Life with Integrity

When I was in my early thirties, I decided to take up the game of golf. During my first year on the golf course, my scores were sometimes almost twice as high as those of some of my playing partners. Since I was the ultimate perfectionist, I was extremely embarrassed. As we called out our scores after each hole, I would be tempted to lower my score by one or two strokes so that it would not sound quite as bad as it was. A tempting voice inside of me would say, "Make up a number. They probably can't count that high anyway." I would think about it and finally answer the voice, saying, "But I would know it, and I am the one who has to live with myself."

What does integrity mean to you? In the case of my golf score, I considered integrity to be an honesty issue. Although honesty contributes to integrity, there are more aspects to integrity than just telling the truth. Integrity is unique for each of us.

As you are thinking about your level of integrity, ask yourself the following questions:

- Do I tell the truth?
- Is my word my bond?
- Do my promises have value?
- Do I do what I say I am going to do?
- Am I committed to commitment?

In my interviews with successful people, I asked them to rate each of the ten strategies on a scale of one to five, where a five indicated that the strategy had contributed significantly to their success. All interviewees rated integrity a five.

In *Golden Nuggets*, Sir John Templeton says, "Probably the greatest secret to peace of mind is living the life of personal integrity—not what people think of you, but what you know of yourself. If you remain true to your ethical principles, your personal integrity can become an attractive beacon for success on every level. Listen carefully to the inner promptings of conscience and live peacefully."

Personal integrity is of utmost importance to success. It is the foundation on which you can build the person you want to be.

Strategy #9 - Take Time to Enjoy Your Life

It is so easy to become absorbed in one part of life and to become out of balance. We are meant to enjoy life. When we allow ourselves to be out of balance, we become more stressed. As a result, we enjoy life less. This limits our success.

Stopping to "smell the roses" is more than a cliché. It points out the importance of appreciating beauty, human relationships and the things that are most important to us. It offers the opportunity to reflect, to decrease stress and to add balance to our lives. This not only contributes to but enhances any success we may achieve.

Often, when people are diagnosed with terminal illnesses, they begin to think about what they would have done differently in their lives. They think about their priorities and how they have lived. If you knew you had just six months to live and that you would have your health during this time, how would you then live your life? What would you do differently? In contemplating these questions, I made a list of the things I would do:

- I would spend more time with my family and friends.
- I would be more spontaneous.
- I would show more emotions, laugh more, smile more and cry more in front of other people.
- I would take better care of my body through exercise, sleep and nutrition.
- I would not be concerned about what others think of me but about what I think of myself.
- I would record messages about life for my grandchildren.
- I would make myself more available to those in need.
- I would spend less time talking and more time listening.
- I would look for opportunities to engage in anonymous acts of kindness.
- I would open my eyes to the beauty of nature and enjoy witnessing the miracles of creation.
- I would express my love for other people, both in my words and in my actions.

After making this list, I decided that I don't need to wait until I have just six months left in my life to do these things. I can do them now.

Take time now to make your list and to make sure that it is part of your priority list. Then seize the joy of the day, savor each moment as special and appreciate the beauty of life!

Strategy #10 - Continue to Learn

Continuous learning contributes to success, both in a person's career and in life. It is easy to procrastinate the development of a learning plan, especially for those who are living a hurry-up lifestyle. However, no matter how hectic your life is, you will become more successful if you make time to continue your learning. Following are some of the options for incorporating learning into your life:

- Obtain a formal education.
- Attend seminars and workshops.
- Read books, magazines, newspapers and information available on the Internet.
- Enhance your listening skills.
- Listen to audiotapes.
- Learn from life's experiences.
- Challenge yourself with new experiences.
- Work with a personal and/or professional coach or mentor.
- Develop a personal learning plan.

A personal learning plan need not be elaborate; nor does it need to take a long time to develop. Start by reviewing your priorities and goals and determining what you need to know in order to achieve what you want in life. From there, you can decide the best methods for learning that which you need and/or want to know.

Albert Einstein once said, "Education is that which remains when one has forgotten everything he learned in school." That which you learn throughout life contributes to your education and to your success.

By integrating and incorporating the ten success strategies into your life, you will increase your potential for enjoying the success that you seek. The ten success strategies really work! They have worked for me, for the successful people I have interviewed and for those I have coached and mentored. They will work for you, too.

I wish you success!

About The Author

Joan Eleanor Gustafson

An award-winning international speaker, author and consultant, Joan Eleanor Gustafson provides inspiration and life-changing insights to organizations and individuals, who want to live their dreams and maximize their results. She is the author of *A Woman Can Do That! 10 Strategies for Creating Success in Your Life* and *Some Leaders Are Born Women! Stories and Strategies for Building the Leader within You.* She has spoken to more than 3,500 audiences in ten countries. Joan is the founder of Success and Leadership Dynamics (SLD), a consulting company specializing in business strategy, organizational productivity, personal development and leadership. In her role as president of SLD, she works with both large and small companies and with business startups in helping them to achieve their objectives and maximize their potential. Before founding SLD, Joan was a member of the Corporate Marketing Management Committee at 3M where, during her 26 years there, she held international responsibility for multiple functional areas including marketing and sales productivity, e-Business and knowledge management. Joan is on the faculties of Income Builders International, where she teaches marketing excellence, and University of Phoenix, where she teaches graduate-level courses in international management and business.

Joan E. Gustafson
8362 Tamarack Village
Suite 119-226
Woodbury, Minnesota 55125-3392
Phone: 602.882.2648
Toll-free: 877.824.3014
Fax: 602.237.0453
Email: joan@leaderdynamics.com
www.leaderdynamics.com

Chapter 4

Conflict: The Untapped Competency

Susan J. Strong

Susan J. Strong is the founder of Strong Consulting, a management and organization development consulting firm located in Morristown, New Jersey. Sue is known for her ability to help organizations achieve results by developing talent and building the business partnerships and goal alignment necessary to realize success. Her work has been both domestic and international in scope and includes assignments in Europe, Latin America, and China. Ms. Strong has partnered on projects with the *London Business School* and has been quoted in the *Wall Street Journal* for her perspective on the ever-changing business world. She is an expert in team development and conflict resolution and is the only consultant in New Jersey certified in the use of the Conflict Dynamics Profile®. Sue has over twenty years of experience in the field of human resource development with experience as a consultant, facilitator, coach, trainer and speaker.

Understanding Competencies

Before we begin to talk about the significance of *conflict* as a competency, we need to understand what competencies are and the purpose they serve in organizations.

Historically, when we thought about people in relation to their work, we categorized them primarily by their job function, for example, an accountant, a lawyer, a human resource director, or a sales manager. This way of defining people became somewhat restrictive as we realized that the human resource director might have or need skills of persuasion just like the sales manager; or, the lawyer might need to have excellent organizational skills just like the accountant.

In addition, we realized that skills were only one aspect of competence. There were other characteristics that embraced knowledge, attitude, and character such as leadership talent, trustworthiness, concern for quality, drive for success. Over time, these transferable distinctions were used to determine elements of success in a position and/or an organization. They broadened opportunities for transfer and promotion, clarified organizational expectations, and helped shape organizational culture. They provided people with consistent information that could help them recognize areas for personal development, and they became organizational differentiators in competitive markets. They also allowed organizations to maximize their utilization of organization talent in new ways. It wasn't unusual to see "competencies" showing up when writing job descriptions, defining leadership success factors, or planning for progression and succession.

Conflict as a Competency

The competencies that were first defined centered on organizational culture and leadership. They were an extension of the work organizations were doing in defining their corporate visions, missions and values answering the question, "What kind of talent would be needed to drive our organization forward?"

The original 360-degree instruments—one source of competency identification—were initially focused on broad sets of skills and characteristics. *Conflict* would be included, for example, in a cluster focused on interpersonal skill. It was not necessarily identified as *critical* to leadership, team, or organizational success.

As a competency, *conflict* management takes into consideration many other more basic skills: the ability to listen, provide feedback, and deliver a straightforward message. Without skill in the basics, it is very difficult to learn to resolve conflict effectively. Conflict effectiveness is built on our ability to use these skills as well as our attitudes about people and constructive interpersonal relationships.

Without the basics in place, it is very difficult to resolve conflict effectively.

Of course this begs the question, "Why is conflict management so important to consider now?" The answer probably has more to do with how organizations and their employees have evolved. We are moving into a time in business life where people are developing and have developed some of the previously mentioned basic interpersonal skills. We have recognized that relationships are as critical to organizational success as functional job skill. In his book on *Emotional Intelligence,* Daniel Golman gave us permission to look inside ourselves, and consider the significance of self-awareness and emotional strength. This appreciation was not always the case. And the response to conflict is, as we will discuss, a primitive emotional response.

In addition, with globalization there are many situations when people have to get things done in cooperation with people over whom they may not have direct authority. The traditional concept of power and influence based in organizational hierarchy is no longer sufficient as a power base. Disagreement, once managed by pushing it up the organizational chain of command, can no longer be resolved in this way alone. In today's world, employees may have to get work done with those who work for them *indirectly.* Today's power is frequently based in the individual, not solely in the position. The skills of influence, negotiation, and conflict resolution are truly personal skills, not hierarchical.

Globalization has also driven the need for professionals to learn to work with people who have many divergent viewpoints, styles and expectations. Cross-functional, multi-national teams are a breeding ground for conflict; yet our traditional approaches won't work the way they once might have. Indeed, skills such as conflict resolution, often referred to as "soft skills" are frequently the most difficult to learn and yet may be the most essential for competitive effectiveness today. The time has come for conflict *leadership* (not just conflict management) to become a respected and developed competency employees at all levels are required to learn.

Conflict Defined

Traditionally we have considered conflict as an abrasive, difficult interaction between two or more people who don't see things in the same way. The word "conflict" brings to mind the words: Clash! Quarrel! Tension! If I am invited to a meeting and know that Erik from

Team A has strong differences with Sofia from Team B, I am braced for a meeting that will probably include argument and squabble. And, if I believe I am going to be pulled into the fray, their conflict may spill over to me, causing a knot in my stomach. Imagine the manager about to provide an employee with a performance review that is not stellar. Is this to be enjoyed? What about the two employees who are constantly at odds? Every day they are either belittling or avoiding each other. Imagine the impact on the people who sit around them.

If we can move beyond this conventional definition of conflict we begin to open opportunities for reframing the conflictual interaction.

What if I saw Erik's and Sofia's differences as simply a problem that needed to be solved? What if I considered the performance review as a learning opportunity, or the factors regarding my two employees who are at odds as simply a knot that needed to be untangled? Is it possible that my response to conflict would be different? Is it possible I could harness the energy I once saw as negative and turn it into something synergistic? Would I be able to revisit my definition of conflict and see it instead, as merely two people who view things differently? If I could remove the emotional overlay could I release a more creative opportunity?

Rethinking the definition of conflict helps us to refine our attitude which then allows us to use our energy toward a more constructive focus. The conflict situation becomes a conversation of difference or, as we prefer to call it, the *difference discussion.* In this way, conflict becomes more of a link than a rupture.

Conflict and Fear in Today's Corporation

Embracing a redefined attitude toward conflict is easier said than done. To understand this we have to return to primitive conflict responses. In the animal world, fear of potential conflict or danger communicates very valuable information. It provides the animal with a trigger allowing the creature to protect itself. As most of us know, the most primitive response to fear is the "fight-or-flight" response. Human beings have brought this response forward into today's business world. Even though we have more sophisticated thinking mechanisms now, we still resort to this inherent basic response when we are afraid: fight or flee.

How does this manifest itself in today's business world? Think about a meeting scenario where multiple participants are in disagreement. What behavior do you observe? It wouldn't be surprising to see some who are withdrawn, quiet, passive (i.e., flight) and others who are arguing, verbally sparring, maybe even raising their voice or finger-pointing (i.e., fight). What so often happens today in a business conflict situation is that people either pull out and/or pull in, or they argue, attack, and talk at and/or over each other.

Unfortunately, while these fight-or-flight behaviors may have helped our ancestors to survive, in today's business world they only create more conflict or cause the conflict to simmer, unaddressed. Smoothing over an issue doesn't make the conflict go away—it creates a breeding ground for a deeper, emotional level of conflict. No one is immune—there are many senior level executives who do not want to deal with someone who has a strong difference of opinion.

Because so many of us have not learned how to constructively deal with conflict, it remains an untapped competency. However, as we develop the skill of *conflict leadership* we are able to use conflict as a problem-solving tool that, at worst, results in problem solving and, at best, serves as a catalyst for generating innovative solutions.

The Cost of Conflict

Before investing in the development of any potential breakthrough that will improve how we do work, organizational leaders are usually interested in assessment costs and benefits. Dan Dana of the Mediation Institute has created a method for considering the cost of conflict. In his analysis for manager or professional level employees, Dana asks us to think about a specific conflict situation and consider such factors as:

- The number of people involved in the conflict
- Their salaries
- Organizational decisions that may have been impacted by the conflict
- Estimated reduction in productivity
- Duration of the conflict
- Cost of terminations that may have resulted from the conflict
- Cost time health costs

Dana's methodology provides a structure to use in considering the dramatic cost of conflict, especially when multiple parties are involved. Dana's formula is an excellent starting point for assessing conflict cost. Taking the cost analysis to another level, we can begin to consider the potential that conflict has as a revenue generator when it serves to unlock creativity.

While the cost of conflict is important to consider, so is its impact. Dollars and cents are significant to consider in a world where we continue to look for ways of doing more with less. However, business is also in the midst of a talent war. We struggle to find the best people all over the world to work for our organizations. We see magazine articles that constantly reference criteria used in assessing which is the "best company to work for." We are attentive to developing leadership skills that create organizational environments where people can have impact, grow, and progress in their careers. With talent management so crucial, why would someone choose to work in a company where improperly managed conflict perpetuates poor morale and diminishes influence? Why would a company overlook this powerful differentiator?

It is also important to consider the affect of conflict in impeding productivity. For example, if I am preoccupied with a boss who is always critical of my work, I am probably going to be cautious in how I interact with that person and the risks I am willing to take. Ultimately, I may become more focused on the relationship breakdown than in getting my job done. At the end of the day, when I go home and tell my spouse about my day, my focus is not going to be on my good work—it is going to be on my unsatisfying interpersonal relationship.

Solving the Project Puzzle: The Benefits of Conflict

After considering the harmful side of the conflict coin, we may start to wonder, what's good about it? What are the benefits? This is, of course, the crux of the matter and the opportunity for organizations and their people.

Consider the following scenario: Tom and Erin are managers in two organizational units who have to work together on a regular basis. Tom has been given fifty pieces of a puzzle—let's call it the *Project Puzzle*. Erin has been given fifty different pieces of the puzzle. Erin may think that with her fifty pieces, she can solve the *Project Puzzle* but, guess what—it's a 100-piece puzzle! No matter how many ways Erin reconfigures her pieces, she will never be able to put the puzzle together--she needs Tom. Now, Erin may argue that her fifty pieces are the right pieces. She may talk louder and become argumentative, but it doesn't matter—she still needs Tom's pieces.

As Erin continues to argue, Tom backs off. He doesn't like to argue so he withholds his *Project Puzzle* pieces. While Erin fights, Tom flees. And the *Project Puzzle* will not get solved because these two people are experiencing disruptive conflict in their interactions.

Now let's assume Erin and Tom are joined by Ava and Matteo. In this scenario Erin has twenty pieces, Tom has twenty-five pieces, Ava has forty pieces and Matteo has the remaining fifteen pieces. Erin continues to dominate and demands her pieces are the most important. Ava is from another culture where she learned to wait her turn and strive for harmony. She sits back and watches. Matteo believes his pieces aren't as important as anyone else's, especially since Erin is so strong. Tom is again withdrawn because of his previous negative interaction with Erin. Erin may assertively push her pieces on everyone else, but she still needs the others to help her solve the *Project Puzzle*. However, the lack of participation from the others on the team is going to prevent them from solving the *Project Puzzle*.

If we could turn this situation around and lead a *"difference discussion,"* we might see the following benefits to conflict:

1. It helps us understand the other person's frame of reference, i.e., where he or she is coming from,
2. It encourages us to pool our resources,
3. It allows for a learning dialogue,
4. It forces cooperation,
5. It results in a better, more complete and synergistic outcome.

Tom, Erin, Matteo and Ava reconvene and are finally able to listen to each other and learn from each other. As they eliminate their fight-or-flight behavior they begin to have a *difference discussion* centered on solving the *Project Puzzle* together.

Conflict, the untapped competency, encourages each of us to begin to think that while I have one point of view and you may have another, maybe I need to understand where you're coming from so we can pool our knowledge; and maybe you need to understand where I'm coming from. Tapping into the energy of both points of view can create a resolution that not only creates win-wins, but is also going to be better for the health and results of our organization.

Different viewpoints are just that—two people (or more) with different ways of looking at a situation. There is much to learn, and much to share.

Leading Conflict: Conflict Styles

Ken Tomas and Ralph Kilman developed a well-known conflict tool in the 1970s. The Thomas-Kilman Instrument (TKI) looks at individual conflict styles as a means of helping people understand different approaches to conflict. Specifically, when conflict arises, we can look at someone's behavior based on his or her *assertiveness* and *cooperativeness*. Thomas and Kilman defined five conflict-handling modes commonly used to deal with conflict in those situations. Each mode is useful when used appropriately. The five modes and their usefulness are as follows:

Competing

Assertive and uncooperative—This is useful when one is defending their position or standing up for their rights.

Accommodating

Unassertive and cooperative—Accommodating individuals will put their needs aside to satisfy the others' concerns. One would use this when they are obeying an order or giving in to someone else's point of view.

Avoiding

Unassertive and uncooperative—Avoiding individuals are those who are not immediately satisfying their needs or the other person's needs. One would use this when it is better to postpone an issue or to withdraw from a threatening situation.

Collaborating

Assertive and cooperative—Collaborating individuals are working to find a solution that will satisfy all parties. This is useful when exploring a disagreement to learn from each other's perspectives or resolving an issue that would lead to more problems.

Compromising

Asertive and cooperative—A compromising individual wants to find a solution that is mutually acceptable. It is useful when seeking a quick middle ground position, splitting a difference or exchanging concessions.

An individual is not characterized by having one mode and a rigid style of dealing with conflict. Some modes may be used more than others and therefore these modes may seem comfortable to us. The behaviors that one uses to deal with conflict come from both personal predispositions and the context of the situation. In learning how I tend to manage conflict, and recognizing that someone else may approach it differently, I can begin to think about when my approach to conflict is: 1) appropriate to the situation and 2) how to be adaptive to work more effectively with the other person.

For example, if Erin is “Competing,” Tom is “Avoiding,” Ava is “Compromising,” and Matteo is “Accommodating,” as a team they have multiple, natural tendencies in how they approach conflict. If Erin recognizes she tends to be aggressive and uncooperative, and she often tries to bully others, it gives her an opportunity to become more collaborative. She might do this by asking more questions or listening more effectively. On the other hand, someone like Tom may need to assert himself more to ensure that he is sharing his very important perspective with the rest of the team—to withhold it would be unfortunate both for Tom as well as the others.

Therefore, as we reflect on how to become more effective in dealing with conflict, we will also want to consider learning to recognize the appropriateness of our conflict styles and how to be adaptive in our style choice when interacting with others in a *difference discussion.*

Maximizing Conflict: Developing Positive Behaviors

Up to this point we have been talking about *reactions* to conflict situations. Reaping the reward of the conflict gold mine occurs when we maximize the outcome of conflict. And the way we do this is by understanding our behaviors and deliberately using those that will help us to achieve optimal outcomes.

When we talk about Style, we are really talking about a label for a collection of behaviors. But to truly maximize the result, we need to dig deeper and understand the concept of behavior and how to use it in our favor.

What is behavior? First of all, it is a choice. My behavior is not genetic—it is more likely to be a learned response to a specific trigger. Behavior is also observable—I can identify it when I see it. Behavior is objective. For example, if I were to tell you that you are doing a “good” job in the way you were handling an ongoing conflict, would you know what I meant? But if I said that you listened, paraphrased, and reflected on what the other person had to say, you would now know the specific behaviors I found to be appropriate. This allows you to identify what has worked and use it again. When we can identify positive conflict behaviors we can choose to use them as opposed to calling on negative conflict behaviors.

In dealing with conflict, we want to move away from fight-or-flight behaviors and identify those behaviors that are most likely to have a positive effect on the conflict situation. What are the behaviors that impact conflict in a positive way, and what are the behaviors that may be more problematic?

Research has been done at the Eckerd College Leadership Development Institute regarding this very issue. Working with a model called the Dynamic Conflict Model (figure 1), they have mapped out a path for dealing with conflict in a way that clearly demonstrates *Hot Buttons, Constructive Responses to Conflict*, and *Destructive Responses to Conflict.*

While this model takes into account several aspects of the conflict response, a critical component has to do with constructive/destructive responses and active/passive responses. As quoted from their material on the Conflict Model: "Responses to conflict also differ in terms of how active or passive they are. Active responses are those in which the individual takes some overt action in response to the conflict or provocation. Such responses can be either constructive or destructive; what makes them active is that they require some overt effort on the part of the individual. Passive responses, in contrast, do not require much in the way of effort from the person. In fact, they typically involve the person deciding to refrain from some kind of action. Again, passive responses can be either constructive or destructive—they can make things better or they can make things worse. Given, then, that responses can be either constructive or destructive, and either active or passive, we view responses to conflict as falling into one of four categories: Active-Constructive, Passive-Constructive, Active-Destructive, and Passive-Destructive."

Figure 1:

conflict dynamics profile®
Path of Conflict*
PRECIPITATING EVENT AND/OR HOT BUTTONS
INITIATE CONFLICT
CONSTRUCTIVE RESPONSES
Behaviors which keep conflict to a minimum
DESTRUCTIVE RESPONSES
Behaviors which escalate or prolong conflict
TASK-FOCUSED CONFLICT (Cognitive)
•Focus on task and problem solving
•Positive affect
•Tension decreases
•Group functioning improves
PERSON-FOCUSED CONFLICT (Affective)
•Focus on personalities
•Negative emotions (anger, frustration)
•Tension increases
•Group functioning decreases
CONFLICT DE-ESCALATES
CONFLICT ESCALATES
*Used with Permission Eckerd College Leadership Developmenvt Institute

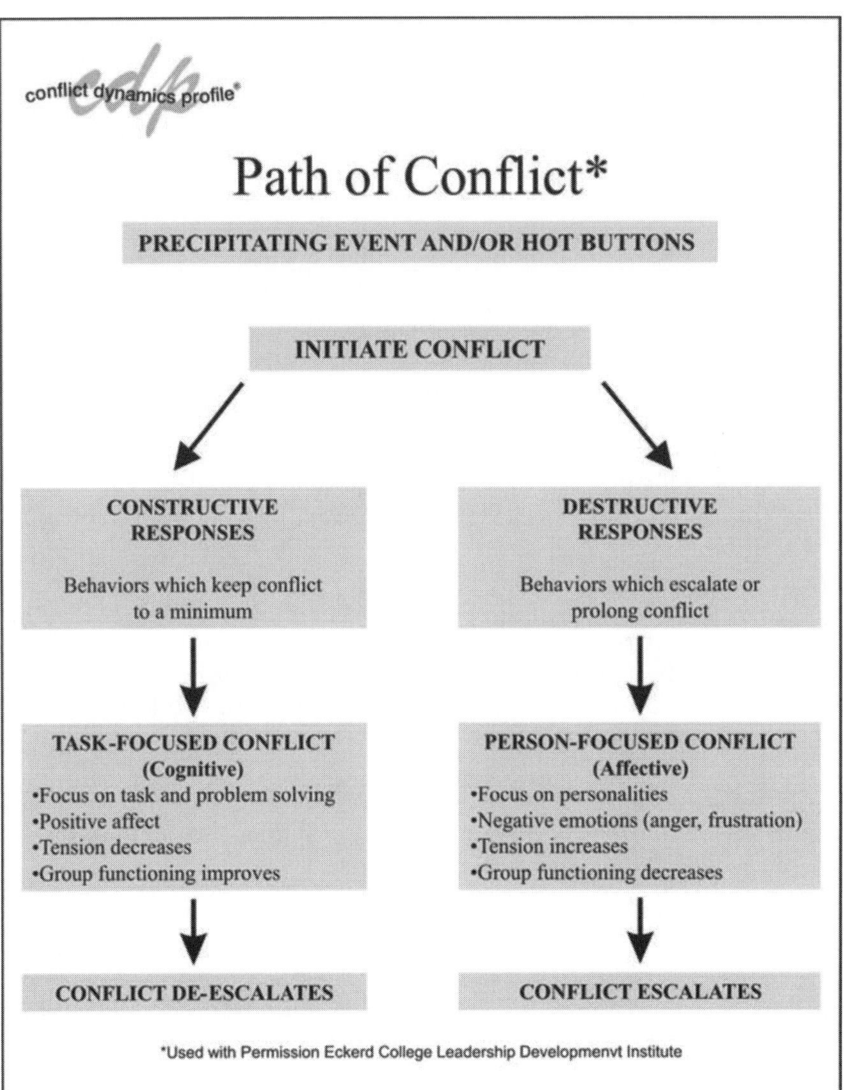

The specific behaviors identified in Eckerd's *Conflict Dynamics Profile* are:

Active-Constructive Response Profile

Four ways of responding to conflict which require some effort on the part of the individual, and which have the affect of reducing conflict are: Perspective Taking, Creating Solutions, Reaching Out, and Expressing Emotions.

Passive-Constructive Response Profile

Three ways of responding to conflict which have the affect of dampening the conflict, or preventing escalation, but which do not require any active response from the individual are: Reflective Thinking, Delay Responding, and Adapting.

Active-Destructive Response Profile

Four ways of responding to conflict which, through some effort on the part of the individual, have the affect of escalating the conflict are: Winning at All Costs, Displaying Anger, Demeaning Others, and Retaliating.

Passive-Destructive Response Profile

Four ways of responding to conflict which, due to lack of effort or action by the individual, cause the conflict to either continue or to be resolved in an unsatisfactory manner are: Avoiding, Yielding, Hiding Emotions, and Self-Criticizing.

As we learn to be more deliberate in our behavioral choice in the *difference discussion,* we become even more adept at leading others and ourselves through conflict.

Getting Started: Tapping into Positive Conflict

When we accept that there is good to be gained from leading conflict, understanding the appropriateness of our style tendencies, and realize there are behaviors that help us to maximize a *difference discussion*, we are left with the question, "How do I apply this knowledge in my day to day work environment?" Here are a few tips for the individual in any organization:

1. Reframe your perspective on conflict—realize it is not a bad thing.

2. Redefine your definition of conflict management to conflict *leadership*. Be proactive in addressing it—think of it as a form of problem solving or creativity.
3. View conflict conversations as *difference discussions* without judgments about right or wrong.
4. Be curious about the other person's point of view—ask questions and explore their perspectives.
5. Don't be afraid of a viewpoint that is different from your own. But, if you are, recognize it is your fear provoking the fight-or-flight response, and make a different choice about how to respond.
6. Enter *difference discussions* as learning opportunities and a way for you to expand your knowledge or attitudes.
7. Accept that in human relationships there will always be differences of opinion and this is quite natural.
8. Learn more about your conflict style and your use of constructive and destructive behaviors. Reflect on and practice new behaviors. By doing this, you will be managing yourself and not allowing destructive behaviors to self defeat you.
9. Learn how to self mediate. When you self-mediate you are practicing how to have *difference discussions* with others that prevent the fight-or-flight response and actually get to the root of issues that may be totally misunderstood by others. This is an excellent way to build relationships and productivity.
10. Remember that the fight-or-flight response is a primitive, non-thinking response and you can learn to conduct yourself in more productive ways.

In addition to the work of the individual, organizations and their managers have an opportunity and responsibility to create environments that are conflict resilient.

Managers need to develop effective mediation skills and model the constructive behaviors they want from their people. Managers also need to take a leadership role in driving a business culture that sees conflict resolution as a positive business opportunity. They need to encourage skills training that will help their people use this competency to their advantage. They need to develop their own skills to create problem-solving and synergistic thinking within their organization.

Finally, organizations need to think about giving their people the tools and developing their people in such a way that they can learn how to manage this very important competency in a productive way. Today's business world is multifaceted and global. By developing conflict *leadership* skills, we can all learn to tap into a competency that has been overlooked as a critical business skill.

Putting it Into Practice: A Brief Case Study

Erik and Marcy are both marketing managers working for two different companies in a co-promote venture. Every time they are in a meeting together they are arguing. Erik works for a small company that moves slowly within a hierarchical decision-making structure requiring organizational consensus. Marcy is part of a large global organization. She has been empowered to make decisions on the spot. Her goal is to move quickly even if things aren't perfect. Erik's goal is to get things right with all appropriate levels of approval. To Marcy, Erik is the problem—slowing things down and not willing to make a decision. In Marcy's eyes they seem to always be rehashing the same issues. To Erik, Marcy is the problem—she is cocky and fast and tends to overlook key details. He is often correcting mistakes she has made due to her drive to just get it done!

Six months into the project, Marcy and Erik are at it again. They are wearing down the patience of their teammates and seem to be arguing purely for the sake of being right. Their managers are concerned that the bickering is impacting the project's success in a detrimental way and have decided to bring in a Conflict Consultant to help Marcy and Erik move past their constant roadblocks.

With the Consultant, Marcy and Erik learn how to problem solve around their differences. They learn that Marcy tends to be assertive and that under stress, this turns to aggression. On the other hand, Erik tends to be cautious. Under stress, he wants to analyze even more. Marcy learns she is good at expressing herself but could do a better job in reflecting before she speaks. She also realizes that she has a tendency to use demeaning behaviors such as sarcasm and eye rolling. She didn't realize this.

Erik can be adaptive but his yielding and avoiding behaviors are problematic. When he realizes he hasn't spoken up or shared his feeling on critical agenda items, he feels the need to continuously revisit previously discussed topics. This cycle has been very detrimental to Marcy and Erik and to the entire team.

As Marcy and Erik learn the skills of self-mediation with their Consultant, they come to appreciate the differences each brings to the team. They learn that their differences, viewpoints, and styles are actually essential for overall success and they develop strategies for supporting each other. Their project ends up winning a marketing award for creativity and Marcy and Erik end up as more effective team players.

About The Author

Susan J. Strong

Susan J. Strong has been working in the field of leadership and organization development for over 20 years. Her experience as a consultant, facilitator / coach, and speaker has provided her the opportunity to work all over the world with highly diverse groups of people. She attributes her success to her deep enjoyment of business and her love of people. At the heart of her work is a belief that has served her well: "Be kind, for everyone you meet is fighting a great battle."
Ms. Strong lives in Basking Ridge, New Jersey with her wonderful husband, Ron.

Susan J. Strong
Strong Consulting
21 Benedict Crescent
Basking Ridge, NJ 07920
Email: sjstrong@strongconsulting.biz
www.strongconsulting.biz

Chapter 5

A Bearable Lightness of Being—
The Magic of Personal Growth

Diane Brandon

If you always do what you always did, you'll always get what you always got.

—*Attributed to Moms Mabley*

Joanne was nervous, smoking one cigarette after another. She was worried about making the wrong decisions, worried about whether others would approve of what she thought or did— worried about almost everything. She didn't like where she was in her life, but she was scared to move forward—or to even move at all....

Dissolve to several months later: Joanne is relaxed, smiling broadly and confidently. She exudes an air of vibrancy and well-being and is obviously strongly in command of herself. No longer afraid to make a move, she has made several positive changes in her life.

What happened?

In those intervening months, Joanne went through some growth experiences and found herself reaping positive rewards.

"Personal Growth." If you haven't yet heard that phrase, no doubt you will at some point in the not-too-distant future. Personal growth, I strongly believe, is one of the waves of the future—and that's not hyperbole!

So what is "Personal Growth?"

Is it the extra pounds we gain as we get older? Or the higher income we receive with that new promotion? Or the increase in family size after we marry?

Nope, it's none of the above.

Personal growth is growth that occurs on the *inside* of us, rather than on the outside (although it can indeed then radiate outward and positively affect those aspects of our lives).

If I were to attempt to define "personal growth," I would define it as a personal process by which we remove self-limiting behaviors, attitudes, beliefs, and habits, thereby enlarging our vision, developing our potential, expressing more of the fullness of our being, and attaining more fulfillment.

Notice that I wrote, "*self-limiting* behaviors, attitudes, beliefs, and habits" in my definition. In other words, it's growing in a positive way, not a negative way.

Personal growth is also a way by which we bring our outer persona and inner realm more in alignment with each other.

Because it's growth in a very personal—intimately personal—way, it's growing on the inside, where the deepest parts of our being reside. In fact, it's any change we go through that enables us to feel better about ourselves—and others—where we can feel that sense of well-being throughout every pore of our being and all aspects of our lives, both inner and outer.

We may think that increasing our knowledge by educating ourselves more and more is personal growth. Well, acquiring knowledge *is* growth, definitely a desirable thing to do. And, in our increasingly complex world with its continual progress in technology and the ongoing information explosion via research in various fields, acquiring knowledge is more and more of a necessity, so that we may keep abreast of advances and weave them into our everyday lives and our work.

But acquiring knowledge is not the "Personal Growth" I'm referring to.

Interestingly, the truth is that we can grow in knowledge without growing personally. Just as we can learn new facts without actually *experiencing* the reality of what we've studied. And many of us do indeed add to our base of knowledge while remaining somewhat entrenched in our attitudes and behaviors.

This is so because gaining knowledge affects us on the *cognitive* level, whereas Personal Growth affects us on the level of our psyches—our emotional and psychological selves—in the deeper levels of our being. It gets us "where we live."

And because Personal Growth gets us where we live, it often precedes positive changes in the external areas of our lives. In fact, Personal Growth not only precedes those positive effects, it can actually help *bring about* improvements in the outward expression of our lives, in our relationships, for example, or our careers. When this happens we often find ourselves more in balance.

Oddly enough, we can also do practically the opposite. We can be quite accomplished in the eyes of the world as a result of having focused on strengthening the outer areas of our lives (career, activities, etc.) and yet not be growing personally (just as we can be quite learned, but not be growing personally).

We can be high achievers and still not feel fulfilled. In actuality, we can be successful in many external ways in our lives and yet still be somewhat impoverished, conflicted, or frustrated on the inside. History is rife with examples of well-known achievers whose inner Achilles' heels brought them down. And many of us may be able to think of contemporary examples of highly successful people in business, in religion, in politics, etc., whose unresolved inner "stuff" was revealed publicly to be in stark contrast with their outer personas and achievements.

In cases such as these, we find ourselves very much out of balance, somewhat like the beautiful palace with the crumbling foundation. Whereas we may think those crumbling foundations are hidden from view, in reality at some point the beautiful palace we have focused on building may come tumbling down. Inner beauty—and inner reality—is just as important as outer beauty and serves as a foundation for it.

However we don't have to be a public figure, have "crumbling foundations," or be tremendously out of balance to benefit from Personal Growth. Whether prince or pauper, CEO or mailroom clerk, teacher or student, physician or therapist, we can all reap the positive rewards of Personal Growth. Nor do we have to be hugely frustrated or stressed. Gains can be made no matter where our starting point is.

It is Personal Growth that allows us to grow on the inside and unfold in a positive way, bringing the different areas of our lives into alignment and thus allowing us to find more true fulfillment in life.

Think Back...

Let's try an experiment. Think back to when you were twenty-one and what you were like then. Have you changed since then?

Now, how about at thirty? Can you see ways in which you've changed?

Okay, are those changes positive? Are you happier now, or more fulfilled? Are you more confident or less stressed?

The point I'm making is that Personal Growth brings about *positive* changes, in who and how we are. And, whereas it is sometimes a by-product of getting older—through gaining insight and maturity over the years from life experiences or from clearing out any outmoded qualities that no longer serve us, like cleaning out our inner closet, we can both speed up that process and ensure more of it by a conscious focus on it.

If you think of your inner being—your mind, thoughts, beliefs, attitudes, etc.—as a garden, it is easy to see that it needs ongoing maintenance. Just as we maintain a garden by watering it, fertilizing it, pruning any dead or nonproductive stems, improving the soil, removing any unattractive foreign matter like choking weeds, leaves, or other debris, planting healthy, desirable new specimens, etc.—all done with a view to strengthening what we're growing in our garden—so too do we need to tend our inner being by removing that which no longer serves us (for example, fears that serve as metaphorical weeds) and planting beneficial inner flora.

Just as a well-tended garden exhibits beauty and healthy specimens, so too does a well-tended mind and psyche. Maintaining our inner being results in healthy and attractive growth, so that our inner beauty may radiate outward. And we inevitably reap positive rewards of our internal gardening: Personal Growth that can benefit us in many ways.

There are so many potential positive effects of Personal Growth that it would be impossible to list them all. So I'll list just *some* positive effects below:

- More Confidence
- More Happiness
- More Fulfillment
- More Understanding (of Self and Others)
- Better Concentration
- More Patience
- More Whole Brain
- More Balanced
- More Creativity
- Better Social Skills

- More Assertiveness
- Better Health
- More Self-Awareness and Self-Acceptance
- More Acceptance of Others
- More Empowered
- More Initiative
- More Proactive
- More Courage
- More Considerate
- More Perceptive
- Better Decision-Making
- More Personal Responsibility
- More Optimism
- More Compassion
- More Tolerance
- More Youthful
- Better Self-Image
- Clearer Perception and Judgment
- Better Relationships

And less of what we don't want:

- Less Fearful
- Less Stressed
- Less Worry
- Less Anger
- Less Negativity
- Less Judgmentalism
- Less Rigidity
- Less Stagnation
- Less Premature Aging
- Less Closed Down
- Less Brusque
- Less Addictions
- Less Impatient
- Less Subjective
- Less Tunnel Vision
- Less One-Sided
- Less Negative Thinking

Now, you have to admit that that's a very impressive list (and a partial one at that!). *And* it's a perfectly realistic list. We really *can* grow in positive ways personally.

And I'm a prime example.

When I think back to how I was at age twenty-one and at thirty, I see someone who was so unsure of herself that she was always looking outside of herself for validation.

I see someone who was seemingly an inveterate people-pleaser, entrenched in her insecurity—full of energy, but never fulfilling her dreams or being truly in command of herself.

I have gone through a lot of growth since then, some of it spontaneous and some of it deliberately cultivated. I can see without qualification that I am a much happier, confident, secure, independent, and fulfilled person now.

I have seen similar results in many of my clients.

My work is directed at facilitating personal growth in others. It's not something I ever planned on doing. In fact, I wasn't even thinking of Personal Growth when I started doing intuitive counseling (*another* thing I hadn't intended to start doing). *And*, if truth be told, had it not been for my own growth and unfolding, I would never have attempted to do intuitive work.

It was only because I had gained more self-confidence that I allowed myself to even consider whether I could do that type of work when it was suggested to me. Academic achievement? Yes, that I knew I could do. And creativity? Yep, that too was a piece of cake. But intuition? Oh, I didn't think so!

You see, it had never been part of my self-image. And I was very much a slave back then to what my self-image was—and letting that dictate what I thought I could do.

Because of the shifts I had already gone through, however, I knew to allow myself to carefully consider, when presented with the prospect of a new activity, whether it was something I could do, rather than react with my old knee-jerk response of "I can't." (Ever hear yourself or someone close to you routinely saying or thinking, "I can't?")

After I allowed myself to admit that perhaps I *could* explore doing that kind of work and after I began to actually do it—quite tentatively at first—I discovered, albeit after many, many months, that I could indeed do intuitive counseling. Not only could I do it, I was also apparently quite good at it, judging by the feedback I consistently received. And it was work that allowed me to feel good about myself, because I was helping others.

I found that developing my intuition and using it on a regular basis was giving me strong personal rewards. I gradually began to incorporate my inner voice and knowing into my everyday life, which not only strengthened me but also gave me significantly more confidence (one reason why I facilitate this in others). In addition to those gains, allowing myself to explore doing intuitive counseling also led to my beginning to speak, write, and teach seminars and workshops on personal growth topics.

I did not set out to focus on facilitating Personal Growth in others. It took a few years, but my counseling work naturally evolved toward that—initially just through counseling, and then through writing and speaking.

And it was only after it evolved that way that I started thinking more consciously about Personal Growth. After watching many of my clients unfold so positively, I began to focus more deliberately on facilitating others' process. As a result, I have seen repeated proof that Personal Growth can bring about incredibly positive things for people in their lives.

I have seen some clients go from being frustrated and unhappy to exuding confidence and feeling in control of their lives.

For example, I have seen others who were quite tense and brusque and not exactly the warmest people in the world become more relaxed, accepting, positive, and heart-centered.

Some have begun to build careers that suit them perfectly, where they can shine, enjoy themselves, and express their true selves.

Future Shock

Interestingly, my delving into Personal Growth—both personally and in my work—dovetailed with many people in our society doing exactly the same thing.

For decades, there have been those who studied and were involved with the "human potential" movement. However, whereas in the sixties the human potential movement—just like yoga and meditation—may have been considered to be on the fringe, today we find more and more mainstream folks embracing the goal of Personal Growth.

And is there any wonder why?

We live in very stressful times. From increased violence and crime, to crowded urban conditions with its traffic gridlock, to pollution and environmental concerns, to higher divorce rates, to terrorism, let's face it: we live in very difficult times.

And many believe that it's our personal "stuff"—those unresolved negative "issues" or shortsighted lack of vision, for example—that contributes to negativity on a large scale—and to those manmade ills that we seem to be seeing more and more of today.

Can you imagine the positive effects of people becoming less stressed? Or more fulfilled? Or more understanding?

Hmm, nice thought, huh?

I personally would love to imagine a world in which more people were fulfilled, peaceful, and happy. What would happen to the crime rate then?

Now, if you agree with me that Personal Growth is a positive thing and a goal to strive for, you may be wondering what it is that keeps us from it?

The answer to that question is that there may be as many individual reasons as there are people. However, we can distill those reasons into some general areas of resistance.

"Heck, No! I Won't Go!"

The first one is that old bugaboo, fear. Fear of change, to put it simply.

It's one thing to tell someone that he or she could be happier; it's another to say that in order to be happier you have to change in some way.

("Uh-oh, you mean I have to change?")

Yep, change, which can elicit major fear for some.

However, fear of change is often no more than a fear of the unknown.

And many people would seem to prefer to be miserable, rather than have to change in some way, simply because their misery is known and familiar. And the truth is that they're more comfortable with the familiar. Isn't that amazing? They'd actually rather be miserable than run the risk of charting unfamiliar waters on the way to becoming happier.

Wow! Can you believe that? Ironic, isn't it?

And that fear isn't just of what unfamiliar things they might encounter in the world as they unfold—for some it's even fear of themselves.

One of the things I advocate in my work is "going within" through some form of meditation or inner reflection (and in fact, I facilitate guided meditation/imagery, both individually and in groups). And I have consistently seen many, many benefits of going within and many people who have reaped wonderful rewards from it.

However, I met some women years ago who, when exposed to the idea of "going within" and getting to know themselves better by learning what was inside of them, said quite bluntly and vehemently that they didn't want to. "I don't want to see what's down there! I'd be afraid to."

The irony of this attitude is that whatever we're ignorant of—especially within ourselves—can control us, especially our fears. "Men who know themselves are no longer fools," said Henry Havelock Ellis.

One path to growing and becoming more fulfilled is precisely that: learning who we are and truly knowing ourselves including all parts of ourselves.

As Henry David Thoreau exhorted, "Explore thyself. Herein are demanded the eye and the nerve." It is only by bringing all parts of ourselves into the light of day that we can be in the driver's seat of our lives. Better to live consciously and with self-awareness than be driven!

Yes, change does mean meeting the unfamiliar, and we may feel some discomfort around it. As Gail Sheehy wrote, "Growth demands a temporary surrender of security." And we often don't become happier or more fulfilled without some change.

Psychologists have said that human nature contains two conflicting needs: the need for security and the need for exploration. And it can also be our need for security—if it's out of proportion with the need to explore—that can keep us stuck.

One thing for sure, if we stay stuck, we won't move forward. Instead we'll stagnate. "All that is human must retrograde if it doesn't advance"—Edward Gibbon.

"If It Ain't Broke, Don't Fix It"

Aside from the fear that comes from a narrow comfort zone, another source of resistance to Personal Growth comes from a desire to remain the same—in all areas—*ad infinitum.*

Some people want to have the same job, same friends, same ideas, etc.—without adding to them—for the rest of their lives. In other words, their lack of interest in Personal Growth comes from a seeming satisfaction with the status quo, rather than any fear-based resistance to change.

And that's perfectly fine (if we really *are* fine) because we don't want to change simply for the sake of change. Change for change's sake can sometimes represent "throwing the baby out with the bathwater."

However, if our preference for the status quo and staying exactly where we are and have been derives from an unwillingness to entertain any thoughts of evolving and becomes representative of stagnation, it may then be unhealthy. Stagnation has its own problems.

Would you want to drink stagnant water. Or have your blood not circulating throughout your body?

Stagnation and stasis are antithetical to Personal Growth and moving forward. While we don't want to throw the metaphorical baby out with the bathwater by changing what works, neither do we want to cling rigidly to outmoded, limiting ways of being. As with anything else, it's best to find a balance between unnecessary change, simply for change's sake, and stagnation.

"What Will the Neighbors Think?"

The idea of Personal Growth may be off-putting to some people because of a fear of what other people will think. In other words, they may feel that Personal Growth entails admitting there is something wrong with them.

For years, therapy and counseling were considered socially taboo in our society. There was not only the stigma of mental illness; there was also a fear of being seen as having something "wrong" with you.

The concern about what others may think can be self-defeating and self-limiting in and of itself. Aside from the fact that it belies a fear, it also practically guarantees that we will never actualize our potential or ourselves. It further practically guarantees that we'll be followers, rather than leaders or trailblazers, or at the very least free and independent thinkers.

Can you imagine a life proscribed by a concern about what others will think?

I can tell you one thing from my own experience: if I had been strictly concerned about what other people thought, I would never have entertained the thought of doing intuitive counseling. And if I hadn't done that, I would never have gained the knowledge I have about intuition, Personal Growth, developing potential, having more mind power, etc. I would never have written the articles and other published material I've written, nor would I have spoken on the topics I've spoken about, nor taught the seminars, workshops, and classes I've taught.

And I would never have felt fulfilled.

If you're bent on achieving things in your life, how much will you achieve if you feel a need to "run with the pack" all the time? How much more could you achieve if you were bursting with health, vibrancy, confidence, and clear-sightedness—and had with the courage to be your own person?

"What, Me Worry?"

Some people may simply not even be aware that they can grow or that their lives could improve. They may indeed be unhappy or frustrated in their circumstances, but simply may not even realize that improvement is a possibility. Even worse, they may be so inured to their constricting circumstances that they may not even realize they're unhappy or frustrated.

They're just like those goldfish in the small bowl.

The story goes that there were two goldfish in a bowl that was so small there was only room for the two of them to swim in a narrow circle. Round and round in this tight radius they went for months—and years.

One day they received the wonderful gift of being moved to a large pool of water, where there was a huge amount of room. Can you guess what those two goldfish did?

They continued to swim in that narrow, confined circle. Know why?

Being narrowly confined was all those goldfish knew. They were so habituated to their confinement that they couldn't even *see* the greater freedom they were given.

Some of us are so used to the narrow confines of our accustomed reality that we can't imagine anything else. Scary, isn't it?

"The Living Dead"

And yet not changing and evolving as we move through life represents stasis—a living death. Life is flux and change, certainly. We can either flow with it or languish and atrophy.

New research teaches us that one sure formula for aging mentally is not doing or being exposed to new things. Conversely, doing new things—even changing everyday habits such as combing your hair with your non-dominant hand, for example—forges new pathways in the brain and prevents premature mental aging.

"The minute a man ceases to grow, no matter what his years, that minute he begins to be old"

—William James.

I don't know about you, but I'd rather be forging those new pathways!

"Our Choice"

So which will it be: nothing but the old and familiar, even if unpleasant, frustrating, or stultifying. Or the new with its possibility of more fulfillment? Or even if you're presently satisfied, the prospect of even *more* satisfaction? I'd bet that if you're even bothering to read this, you're more inclined to venture toward possible improvement and the promise of a better tomorrow.

And even if you're sitting on the fence about this whole thing, I can tell you one thing: We *can* change. We *can* be happier. We *can* be less stressed. We *can* be more fulfilled. (Okay, that was more than one thing.)

So does it always take major change or constant change? Of course not! Our lives don't need to be turned upside down for us to grow and evolve. We don't have to turn into "drama queens" about growth. Nor do we *always* have to focus on growth. Even working on Personal Growth requires a degree of balance. (No obsessions about growth, please!)

We can be growing and unfolding, while also maintaining a balance in our lives. And we don't always have to completely lose sight of the familiar shore—the landmarks in our lives—to be growing. In other words, it doesn't always have to require a huge leap.

The wonderful thing is that sometimes growth can begin simply by a *willingness to change.*

Or by being more open to new things.

Sometimes just by changing our self-image or by merely seeing more possibilities for ourselves, great shifts can occur. They can also occur by being willing to openly examine a self-limiting belief about our world, others, or about ourselves.

Are there personal attributes that can help bring about Personal Growth? You bet your life there are!

Openness is one of the greatest traits for growth and positive change. If you think about it, being closed down doesn't exactly make for a great culture medium for growth!

Curiosity is another marker. That wonderful quality of childlike wonder that leads us to want to explore our world and each other is a wonderful precursor and trigger of Personal Growth. Add in a dash of willingness to change and a pinch of desire to improve, coupled with a trust in the benevolence of a higher power (God) and—*voilà*—we have the perfect ingredients for the ultimate Personal Growth soufflé.

"Mother, May I?"

So *how* do we grow? What is the actual process of Personal Growth?

Although most of us may have been taught and have believed that we can only learn and grow through pain and difficulty, it is actually true we can grow and unfold through positive means.

Yes, I'll admit that it's true that many times it does take a crisis or trauma—the figurative "dark night of the soul" or proverbial two by four—to get our attention and stimulate growth. The loss of a job, the end of a relationship, or the death of a loved one is, we all know, a sure-fire catalyst for change.

However, the belief that we can grow *only* through pain may be one of the reasons why we may want to avoid growth. And it's an erroneous belief.

I repeat: we can grow and change and improve through positive means. Something as simple as learning a new skill, perhaps something we've always wanted to do—taking up painting or a new sport, for example—can give us greater confidence and a new perspective.

More and more people are learning the benefits of Personal Growth. Because of this, we can increasingly find those who specialize in facilitating growth in others. The tools and methods available grow in number all the time as well as new modalities are continually being created.

Our pace of growth can vary, as well. Sometimes we may grow slowly and almost imperceptibly, without even working at it. Other times we may grow quite quickly. We may have active periods of rapid, even intense, growth and at other times we may plateau for long periods of time.

There may be times when we have a sense of something in us "coming up" to be looked at and worked on, or perhaps cleared and released. When this happens, we may then seek out the appropriate practitioner to facilitate the growth or healing.

"Divine discontent" is a phrase being used more frequently to refer to that general sense of discomfort or unease which signals to us that we're ready for some change or that we're on the cusp of a new phase in our lives.

And sometimes our "gut" will be telling us we need to do something, even if we have no inkling at the time as to why it's important or what role it may play. If we follow that thread, what we are drawn to will often turn out to be instrumental in some way in the process of our unfolding.

For example, one client kept feeling like taking a course on photography, even though she didn't know what it would contribute to her process. Several months later, after having taken the course, she discovered that it turned out to be an essential element in a positive new direction she took.

You see, no matter how we go about it, we *can* grow in a positive way.

We can even grow without being in turmoil.

We can grow and unfold while also being centered and calm, becoming the eye in the hurricane while the storm may be raging around us.

Is it true that we can grow personally without *ever* feeling uncomfortable? Not really. There will likely be times when we'll feel some discomfort, perhaps when we enter that unknown realm. As Gail Sheehy wrote, "With each passage of human growth we must shed a protective structure (like a hardy crustacean). We are left exposed and vulnerable—but also yeasty and embryonic again, capable of stretching in ways we hadn't known before." That discomfort, however, is temporary and is quickly replaced by the greater satisfaction that the fruits of growth bring.

And as we continue to grow and unfold, we can become even more open to that process of change. Like a well-developed muscle, it becomes easier and easier to use and with less effort.

If we have done a large amount of Personal Growth, does that we mean that we'll never go through difficult times?

No, not really. Growing personally is no guarantee that we'll live completely charmed lives. Life being what it is, it is almost impossible to live without encountering some personal difficulties or tragedies from time to time—the illness or death of a loved one, career ups and downs, even a storm or disaster of nature.

What Personal Growth *does* give us are the inner reserves and resilience to move through personal difficulties or pain more easily and less painfully. We may not be completely impervious to whatever the difficulty may be, but we'll not be completely bent down by it either. The more open and experienced we are with growth, the more gracefully and quickly we can navigate those distressing straits when they do appear in our path. And the more quickly or easily we can come out on the other side.

A Bearable Lightness of Being

As we grow, we often begin to feel lighter and more optimistic. Life can become easier and more enjoyable, as we continue to discover new pleasures and new ways of being.

And the wonderful thing about Personal Growth is that it doesn't just benefit us. It has its rewards and benefits for those around us as well. Have you ever spent time around a genuinely positive person? If so, have you noticed the positive effect just being around them had on you? Believe it or not, scientific research shows that those around us physiologically affect us.

Research by the Institute of HeartMath shows that the type of emotions people feel have an actual physiological effect on others in close physical proximity. Think about that one for a moment. Negative emotions will impact others negatively and positive emotions the opposite. And these effects aren't just limited to families or friends. We will impact anyone in close proximity to us.

There's an implication for the workplace as well.

Whenever we're feeling somewhat negative from our personal problems or are even feeling a little frustrated or disenchanted, that negativity will affect our co-workers.

It also affects our work quality as employees when we're dealing with problems or feeling frustrated. We all know that low morale, tension, and misunderstandings can affect productivity. Without a doubt, employees bring their personal problems, concerns, mindsets—and corresponding less positive emotions— to work.

Aside from low productivity or work errors, low morale can also lead to conflicts with others—and teamwork goes out the window.

Happily, the converse is also true. The positive effects of Personal Growth can raise morale, resulting in fewer errors, better decision-making, and higher productivity. Without exception, any time we're experiencing positive growth that allows us to feel more positive, others will feel the positive effects of our growth—and businesses will reap the rewards that result.

Conflict with others can go down and conflict resolution can be expedited or even become obsolete. Teamwork can be improved. Creativity can be developed and achieved, with payoffs in Marketing, Human Resources, research and development, etc. Even long-range planning can reap the rewards of employees' Personal Growth. Continuous improvement can become a commonplace and everyday reality.

And if you regard each business as a microcosm or a cell within a greater organism, imagine those positive effects of Personal Growth spreading out to society as a whole. Nice thought, isn't it?

So, what do you have to lose in embracing Personal Growth?

Your stress? Frustration? Discontentment? (Would you really miss them?)

What new vistas lie waiting for you to discover?

What new experiences and joys can you savor as you fly unencumbered from the shed cocoon of any self-limitations?

So indulge yourself. Allow yourself to tend your inner garden. The resulting fulfillment you gain can become contagious!

Growth is exciting; growth is dynamic and alarming. Growth of the soul, growth of the mind!

—Vita Sackville-West

About The Author

Diane Brandon

Diane Brandon is an Intuition Expert and Personal Growth and Mind Power Facilitator who speaks on Intuition, Creativity, and Dreams and conducts seminars on Demystifying and Developing Intuition, Maximizing Creativity, and The Art of Listening. In our contemporary, fast-paced, and stressful world, being able to keep pace with change while also being centered, clear-eyed, and calm is becoming increasingly important—and indeed it's more and more critical in the workplace. Diane has been empowering and facilitating clients to find their center, while also helping them to garner more fulfillment, self-awareness, and confidence in their lives for over twelve years. And she loves catalyzing others to tap into their unused consciousness potential.

Diane Brandon
P. O. Box 233
Cordova, TN 38088-0233
(901) 752-5052 Voice Mail
(901) 754-2935 Fax
Email: dianebrandon@bellsouth.net
www.dianebrandon.net

To Book Diane for Seminars and Keynote Speaking, Contact:
Theresa Waltermeyer
Antico Internationale
112 Fenton Drive
Carney's Point, NJ 08069
(856) 299-0384
Fax (856) 299-0387
Email: Theresaw@anticousa.com

Chapter 6

Turbo-Charge Your Memory

Your Most Valuable Asset

Nita Scoggan

Do *you* want to be a millionaire?

When I ask an audience that question there is always a loud response—I've heard them shouting: "Me!" "I do, I do!" "Yeah!" or "Me, too, over here!" Most hands are stretched up high. Some people stand up and wave their hands, as if I were Santa Claus, ready to give away big bucks.

I always tell the crowd, "I've got good news for *you*! There is plenty of money for everyone!"

After the applause, I caution: "Now for the bad news. Not everyone is going to be a millionaire because of poor health and memory problems. We spend billions on health care yet Americans have more heart attacks, diabetes and Alzheimer's than many third world countries. Money can't prevent health or memory problems. But, I have more good news! Are you ready?

If you listen to the cutting edge information I'm going to share—and act on it—you'll be healthy and able to earn, and enjoy, a million dollars!

Don't overlook causes of poor health, even when you're young. What you discover in these pages will help you find answers to:

1. What causes health and memory problems?

2. What you can do to prevent memory loss?
3. How can you boost your brain and avoid the risk of future loss of wealth and happiness?
4. Where can you find the nutritional products you need?

1. WHAT CAUSES MEMORY and HEALTH PROBLEMS?

A. STRESS—Stress is caused by pressure placed on us by the demands of others, such as: military training or combat, the pressures of learning a new job or working for a demanding boss.

Stress is caused by the demands we place on ourselves, such as: striving for all A's in college, providing finances for a family, or living life as a perfectionist. Stress is caused by grief, anger, jealousy, and depression. Stress is also caused by life situations such as: death of a loved one, divorce, marriage problems, pregnancy, loss of a job, major illness, retirement, a large mortgage, long vacation or relocation.

How we handle situations and the stress in our life affects our physical and mental health.

Why is eliminating stress so important to our health? Because stress can kill. Heart attacks, strokes, and other diseases can be caused by stress. In the October 2003 *Woman's World* magazine article, "Staying Young and Healthy," author Caitlin Castro stated: *"Doctors say stress is now our number one health problem and estimates it contributes to as many as ninety percent of all doctor visits"* (p.36).

Stress causes memory loss! When your body is under stress it produces cortisol as well as adrenalin. The greater the stress the more cortisol is produced by your body. This disrupts short-term memory. In his book, *The Omega RX Zone*, Dr. Barry Sears states: "... *Nothing kills brain cells faster (especially...where memories are stored) than excess cortisol"* (p. 42).

B. WHAT YOU EAT—What you eat can cause memory and health problems. Is there a connection between food and memory loss? Some scientists acknowledge that healthy lifestyles help lower the risk of Alzheimer's disease. In the January 19, 2004, edition of *Newsweek,* the article "Now, Reduce Your Risk of Alzheimer's," by Anne Underwood reported on newly published studies showing a correlation between food choices, obesity and memory loss. So, therefore, it is wise to cut down or avoid these memory thieves:

- Refined Carbohydrates such as: potatoes, pasta, bagels, candy, donuts and soft drinks made with sugar these make your brain sluggish.
- Hydrogenated or partially hydrogenated fats found in cookies, crackers and other bakery goods.
- Sugar: The USDA Food Pyramid daily nutritional guide contains two cups of sugar! Your insulin levels rise with sugar intake. High insulin levels are associated with tumor growth. Excess blood sugar gives the best environment for cancer.

  Dr. Nicholas Perricone states: *"Sugar reacts with chemicals in our bodies which is why diabetics age one third faster than other people when their sugars are poorly managed." The Perricone Prescription 2002,* (p. 34).

  In the January 2003 *Newsweek,* Geoffrey Crowley states, *"Americans have grown sicker and fatter since the USDA Pyramid came out a decade ago"* (p. 46).
- Processed Cheese—Dr. James F. Balch warns that processed cheese used in fast food sandwiches, has a high aluminum content. The addition of aluminum gives the cheese its melting quality, and aluminum is absorbed in your brain. Look for "processed cheese" on package labels. *Prescription for Nutritional Health, 2000* (p.88).

C. WHAT YOU DRINK can cause memory problems:

- Fluoride—Dr. William C. Douglas warns of Fluoride in tap water, *"In Scandinavia, Europe and in nearly every other medically advanced nation, they have banned the practice of fluoridation...Because fluoride makes your body absorb extra aluminum and where does the aluminum go? Your brain."* (*Health Newsletter, Fluoride,* p. 3). Try to drink only purified water.
- Aluminum—Dr. James F. Balch warns that research has found a strong correlation between aluminum intake and Alzheimer's disease. It's best to avoid aluminum cooking utensils, antiperspirants, drinks in cans, and non-prescription drugs containing aluminum used for inflammation and pain. (*Prescription for Nutritional Health, 2000* (p.87-88).

- Aspartame—is found in diet drinks and food. Recognized as "Equal" and "Nutrasweet." It can cause symptoms that include headache, dizziness and memory loss. Some people are more sensitive to Aspartame than others. Dr. Christine Northrup says, *"Lab studies have proven irreversible brain damage in immature lab animals."* (*The Wisdom of Menopause*, 2001, p. 322.)

D. OVER-THE-COUNTER MEDICATIONS can cause memory problems:

- Diphenhydramine—Is found in many over the counter medications for sleep, colds and allergies. It decreases acetylcholine levels in the brain. Acetylcholine regulates memory, learning and other cognitive functions. Check the labels. Some that contain this drug include Sominex, Benadryl, Tylenol P.M., Excedrin P.M. and Contact Day and Night. (Dr. Christine Northrup, M.D., *The Wisdom of Menopause, 2001*, p.320.)
- Dextromethoraphan—Is found in some cough medicines. This also affects acetylcholine levels in the brain and can impair memory. *(Ibid)*
  Dr. Balch also warns: *"Pre-senile dementia may strike when an individual is in his forties."* (*Prescription for Nutritional Heath, 2000, p.8-9.*)

2. WHAT YOU CAN DO TO PREVENT MEMORY PROBLEMS

- Drink water—it's free! Water wakes up your brain. When your mind gets fuzzy, just before a test or big meeting, drink water—it makes a big difference! Tempted to skip water? Ann Louise Gittleman says: *"Water decreases hunger and keeps the brain alert."(Eat Fat, Lose Weight*, 1999 p. 125). Remember, water makes the difference between a grape and a raisin! Water keeps your brain alert!
- Avoid Dehydration—Dehydration can also cause memory problems. Don't wait until you feel thirsty to drink water. Tea, coffee, juice, milk or even thin soups help hydrate your body. Dehydration is a major problem among the elderly—resulting in confusion, memory loss and other cognitive functions.

- Stop Smoking—Dr. James F. Balch, reported on a study published in the British Medical Journal, *The Lancet,* which stated: *"Smoking more than doubles the risk of developing dementia and Alzheimer's disease"* (p.171).
- Exercise—It's free! It doesn't have to be strenuous to get your blood circulating. It helps "wake up" your brain! There is growing evidence that exercise can enhance memory and slow cognitive decline, when we make it part of our daily routine.

Fred Gage at the Salk Institute has shown that exercise appears to stimulate the growth of nerve cells in the brain. (*Barry Sears, The Omega Zone Diet*, 2002, p.198.)

Dr. Nicholas Perricone says exercise enhances energy on the cellular level which slows down the effects of aging. It strengthens your heart and boosts oxygen to your brain. (*The Perricone Prescription,* 2002, p.143.)

An article in the Newsweek Special Edition, Fall/Winter, 2001 Fighting Back With Sweat), reported on animal studies done at the Institute for Brain Aging and Dementia, by authors Adler and Raymond suggest that exercise enhances memory by promoting the growth of dendrites—communications between brain cells. (p. 36-39.)

Dr. Don Colbert recommends exercising first thing in the morning. Your body has depleted its sugar reserves during the night, so your body will burn fat. More than ninety percent of the people know exercise is good, but only twenty percent exercise! (*Dr. Don Colbert, M.D., What Would Jesus Eat?, 2002,* p.177-180.)

Take a fifteen-minute walk any time. During the day, move everything—swing your arms, lift your legs, do ankle circles, look over each shoulder. Remember, use it or lose it!

3. EAT FOR YOUR PHYSICAL AND COGNITIVE HEALTH

- Eat walnuts, almonds, flax seeds or other nuts—these contain Omega-3, which produce anti-inflammatory substances.
- Use olive oil for cooking and salads to keep arteries open.
- Eat avocados, sardines and pumpkin. These foods contain Omega-3 fats.
- Unrefined Carbohydrates—Beans, peas and brightly colored fruits and veggies, such as: raspberries, blueberries, broccoli, zucchini and green peppers. All of these contain salicylates—substances found in aspirin (Sari Harrar, *Prevention, Jan. 2003, Inflammation: Friendly Fire,* p.113).

Dr. Perricone recommends decreasing carbohydrates and increasing protein. Several nutritionists suggest protein at every meal, if possible—meat, eggs, fish, cottage cheese and any non-processed cheese.

Aim for two fish meals a week. My mother said fish was brain food. It seems research proves that is true. So, be good to yourself.

Dr. Periconne finds that most of us need more Omega-3—essential fatty acids (EFAs) which are found in Salmon and many cold-water fish. He states, *"...fish contains high levels of a substance called DMAE that enhances cognitive function."* (*The Perriconne Prescription,* 2002, p172).

Dr. Bruce West has been seen by more than 30 million people on national television for over three years. In the Summer 2003 issue of *The Journal of Health Discoveries,* Dr. West writes about the alarming percentage of mental and emotional problems caused by the lack of vitamin B complex and Omega-3 fats. He stresses both of these nutrients are crucial for good mental health. Dr. West explains, *"Omega-3 fats are found primarily in fish and flax oil...instead we*

> *load up on Omega-6 fats found in vegetable oils...(which) is bad for your health*" p.5.

Dr. Barry Sears, in his book *The Omega RX Zone,* goes even farther in stating the daily need for Omega-3 fats found in fish oil:

"If you can do only one thing in your life to improve your health, take a daily dose of pharmaceutical-grade fish oil. This type of fish oil can at least partially compensate for a wide variety of lifestyle sins, like eating too many carbohydrates, not exercising enough, not reducing stress, or being overweight... high-dose fish oil has an immediate and direct impact on your eicosanoid levels, and there in lies the key to long-term wellness." p.218

4. HOW TO BOOST YOUR BRAIN AND AVOID RISK OF FUTURE LOSS OF WEALTH AND HAPPINESS

A. Take daily vitamins and supplements—You can't get enough nutrients from the average American diet. You need to read labels on one-a-day vitamins, make sure they contain magnesium, calcium, selenium, B-12 and folic acid. Consider adding Alpha Lipolic Acid – proven to help prevent memory loss.

Dr. Nicholas Perricone, M.D. recommends a super antioxidant—Alpha Lipolic Acid. He states it is, *"400 times stronger than vitamins C and E...it can slow the onset of illnesses such as Alzheimer's disease, heart disease and arthritis...if you are forty or older, I suggest you take at least 100 milligrams a day." (The Perriconne Prescription, 2002, p.134.)* Dr. Perricone prescribed fifty milligrams of Alpha Lipolic Acid, three times a day, for a patient who complained of memory loss, "*...it is also proven to help prevent the onset of cognitive loss.*" (*Ibid*, p. 149.)

Take essential oils (EFAs) supplements. Flax seed oil, Fish oils, Borage oil, and other oils such as Lecithin and vitamin E. Dr. Barry Sears states that Japanese researchers found students under stress of exams have had an increase in mental alertness after taking a high dose fish oil supplement (Lecithin) prior to the exams. (*The Omega RX Zone, 2002*, p.127.) This inexpensive over-the-counter nutrient increased their mental abilities to recall information on tests.

Phosphatydilserine—remember it (fos-fuh-tie-dul-she-reen). It is known as "PS." Green vegetables, soy and rice contain PS, however, the average American only gets a tiny amount, or none, in their diet. Some people don't like veggies, soy or rice.

Caitlin Castro says "New research shows this simple plant extract can pump up your energy, clear away mental fog, boost your mood and more. Getting more PS in supplement form can change our brains for the better." (*Article: Staying Young and Healthy, Woman's World,* 2003 p. 36.) Reporting on the findings of several medical studies, Castro states: *"Scientists at the Memory Assessment Clinic in Bethesda, Maryland report that PS can also improve general learning and memory by 30 percent in three months..."Ibid*

Remarkable Memory Recoveries with PS:

I've had the personal experience with seeing remarkable results in several people, in various stages of memory loss, who took PS. One person took 300 milligrams of PS for three months and began noticeable improvement in alertness, energy and memory. Within a year, neurologists were astounded by the remarkable restoration of cognitive function. Another person no longer recognized her family, couldn't feed or dress herself and spoke almost nothing. She recovered after taking 500 milligrams for six months. She recognized faces and remembered each person's name! She continues to improve and her dose of PS remains at 300 milligrams per day.

A Friend's Experience with Memory Loss and Vitamin B-12:

Joanne wasn't aware anything was wrong!

A person with memory loss may not be aware that anything is wrong with them. That is what happened to my friend—I am changing her name to Joanne. She was a talented executive with a stressful job. She traveled extensively as an official representative for a large organization, giving speeches and writing educational materials. Joanne loved her job; in spite of the long hours, the pay was great and it was never boring.

Joanne noticed that she was having trouble remembering things, so she began writing notes to herself. Because she felt run-down, Joanne went for a checkup. She mentioned the tiredness and forgetfulness, but the doctor found nothing wrong—and suggested more rest.

In the next few months, she lost her train of thought during a speech! It embarrassed Joanne. This happened several times, and it got worse! She totally went blank on one occasion. Even though she had her speech outline in front of her, Joanne couldn't remember what was to be said. She stumbled to an ending, and got off the platform quickly.

After that experience, Joanne's fine support staff typed out every word of a speech for her and she simply read it at the meetings. Meanwhile, she sought another doctor's opinion and another. She was diagnosed with Alzheimer's disease. Joanne said, *"Heart disease or cancer wouldn't have seemed as bad as losing my brain's ability to function."* Her doctors offered little help. Retirement was recommended.

Joanne took two weeks vacation to Florida to decide what to do. While there, she found a medical clinic and went for a checkup. Blood tests revealed very low levels of B12. The doctor recommended daily B12 injections, as well as other nutrient supplements lacking her diet. Joanne continued the injections, feeling energized for the first time in years. She began taking long walks and swimming. Her follow-up was scheduled three months later. Feeling good again, she went back to work.

Joanne still read her speeches and relied on her staff to write them out word for word. However, she took her B12 supplements daily and her memory improved rapidly. Her brain dysfunction disappeared! Six months later, she was offered a promotion and a new job. Today, Joanne operates her own business and according to her *"I feel better every day."*

5. WHERE TO FIND ITEMS YOU NEED

- PS is available at many health-food stores under brand names like *Solgar* and *Source Naturals (Neuro PS).*
- Phosphatydilserine is available at GNC, The Vitamin Shoppe and a few health stores. (Not everyone knows it as PS.)
- Phosphatydilserine can be ordered from vitamin catalogs, often at a good discount. For example:
    - The Vitamin Shoppe – 800-223-1216
    - Puritan's Pride – 800-645-1030
    - Swanson's – 800-437-4148

As always, talk to your doctor before taking any supplement or medication. PS is a soy-based nutrient and has not been found to conflict with prescriptions.

6. FINAL THOUGHTS – TURBO CHARGE YOUR BRAIN

Recognize how valuable time is – everyone has only 24 hours a day. None of us know how many months, days or years we have to achieve our dreams, but we must use our time wisely. You must set aside time by planning your day. Take charge. If you don't plan your time, someone else will. You must make time for exercise, rest and enjoying your family. Time is one of your most valuable possessions.

The information in this chapter can change your life for the better, but only if you apply it. Think about your health, right now. Be honest. Do you need to make some changes? Don't make excuses – instead start investing in yourself and your future wealth and happiness.

You are a powerful role model for your family and those who work for you, or with you. Remember, as a leader, especially as a Christian, your actions speak louder than words. Start today to develop a healthy lifestyle program that will improve your chances to be a millionaire – or achieve your dreams and goals.

7. DEVELOP A TURBO-CHARGED BRAIN LIFESTYLE that consists of:

- Quitting cigarettes.

  Do you have enough self-discipline to quit smoking? You've already read that it will increase your chances of getting Alzheimer's disease by 50%
- Exercising regularly. Start walking, swimming, any type of exercise—just do it.
- Maintaining a moderate weight.
- Eating a high health diet.
- Taking vitamins and supplements daily.
- Drinking lots of water.
- Supplementing your diet with 5 grams (equivalent to 2 Tablespoons or 8 capsules) of Omega-3 fatty acids per day. This must be high-dose pharmaceutical-grade fish oil.

In his book, *The Omega RX Zone,* Dr. Barry Sears, M.D. recommends a plan for developing a "supernormal" brain. It is an exciting program for what I call "turbo-charging" your brain.

Sears' program includes an insulin-controlling diet, exercise and meditation to help you get a good night's sleep. By following his comprehensive program he says, "*You will achieve a 'supernormal' brain, with enhanced cognitive functions that give you an unfair advantage in the world around you.*" p.201

Most of all, he stresses the importance of <u>ONLY</u> using pharmaceutical grade fish oil:

"The most important factor in developing a supernormal brain is adequate dietary supplementation with high-dose pharmaceutical grade fish oil, providing at least 5-10 grams of long-chain omega-3 fats per day. Without that foundation, it will be virtually impossible to improve your brain functioning...", p.200.

Don't lose your winning competitive edge – a quick, sharp- as- a-tack brain. I want to close with thoughts about the importance of our brain, with a quote by Dr. Barry Sears, M.D.

"In summary, your brain is the key to your humanity. It is without a doubt the most valuable asset you have, so treasure it accordingly." *The Omega RX Zone,* p. 127

About The Author

Nita Scoggan

Nita Scoggan is a national keynote, seminar and international conference speaker. She is the award-winning author of 17 books, professional member of the National Speakers Association, respected Adjunct Professor and business owner. With enthusiasm and humor she relates success principles learned in her 25-year career, as a research analyst and illustrator, at the Pentagon. In 2004, Nita was appointed President of the Advisory Board for Oakland City University-Bedford, Indiana. As a member of the OCUB faculty, she teaches Business and Liberal Arts courses. A frequent television guest on national and Canadian programs, Nita stresses the value of education in order to be more successful. From 1973-1993, Nita gave her lunchtime to God by teaching daily prayer and Bible classes at the Pentagon. Her ministry is credentialed by the Department of Defense Armed Forces Chaplaincy Board. In 1984, Nita was invited to the White House to conduct weekly ministry to the White House staffers. For almost 15 years, from Presidents Reagan to Clinton, teaching focused on prayer, believing faith and being doers of the Word. Nita Scoggan is a remarkable woman of faith. Born at her grandmother's home, a 2-pound preemie at birth, the doctor declared she had "no chance to live." But live she did! Placed in a shoebox, fed with an eyedropper–without medical aid–her survival was a miracle. She overcame health problems and poverty, giving God the credit for it all. "I believe in miracles! I've seen them, in answer to prayer. I know God can do anything, so I love to pray," says Nita. Her driving force is to uplift, encourage and empower others to achieve their maximum potential in life. Her motto is "Never give up your dreams-pursue them with patience and persistence."

Nita Scoggan
Maximum Zone Consulting
P.O. Box 2125
Bedford, IN 47421-7125
E-mail: nscoggan@ocub.oak.edu
www.the-maximum-zone.com
To Schedule Nita to Speak
Call 1-866-735-2498

Chapter 7

Living Your Values – Day by Day, Decision by Decision, Action by Action!

The Hidden Key To Personal Integrity and Success

Rick Houcek

The noisy crowd chatters incessantly, finally settles into their auditorium seats, and the roar slowly dies to silence. The mike is tapped for a sound check, and a professionally attired woman glowingly introduces the CEO to the anxiously gathered shareholders. A stately, graying gentleman, impeccably dressed in a pinstriped suit, rises to a thunderous ovation, shuffles papers at the podium, and begins to speak. You could hear a pin drop. Thousands sit in total silence, awaiting critically important information—the financial report, the earnings forecast, and the all-important future plan for success, growth, and stock value increase.

As the CEO speaks, slides filled with charts and graphs illuminate the oversized screen behind him, adding indisputable credence to his words. To the joy of all, his report is a good one—earnings are up, the future looks bright, and the plan for success is solid—any shareholder's nervousness about the safety of his or her investments slowly withers away. The CEO's charisma, charm and believability are off the chart. Unbridled optimism prevails. And the annual state-of-the-company report concludes with a celebration of success.

Fast-forward one year.

Much has changed in the last twelve months, and none of it is good. The company is under investigation for financial fraud. Securities investigators comb the halls and huddle in offices. The CEO, the CFO and several other top company officials and directors all have lawyers who have padlocked their lips. None are talking. They are no longer seen walking the halls being greeted by envious, admiring employees. They are only spotted on the 7 o'clock News, rushing past microphones and cameras, saying nothing, and being whisked away by waiting limousines. Television reports are grim, saying profits have been siphoned for personal use, retirement funds are bare, and bankruptcy looms. Disturbing images burst on-screen, showing corporate jets landing, multi-million dollar homes of top company leaders, and video footage of lavish corporate events costing a king's ransom.

Employees wonder, what does this all mean to me, to my income, to my family, to my kids' college education, to our retirement? The bubble has burst, rumors fly, jobs are in jeopardy, optimism is dead, and anger explodes. "Those guys lied to us" is the prevailing belief—it is company-wide and felt by all.

True story? Or pure fantasy created by Hollywood's finest scriptwriters?

Sadly, you know the answer. This story has been repeated in America's newspapers more times than we can count—on the *front* page where news is told, not in the movie section where make-believe is laughed about.

What's the point of this story? *Values.* Those deeply-held beliefs that drive our decisions and actions... that cause some people to lead lives of high integrity and be admired by all... that push others to criminal behavior leaving them hated, mistrusted and often prison-bound... and leave most teetering somewhere in the middle, committing lesser "values crimes" that irritate and upset others, but aren't worthy of jail time.

The story I just told, and ones like it, disgust me. I'm angered for two reasons. First, a few powerful people made conscious, premeditated decisions that horrendously violated the "greater good" within a company, and second, a large body of people got hurt by those choices.

Leaders involved in those heinous plots should be imprisoned forever, keys hurled into the ocean. They won people's trust under a mask of deceit, and knowingly swindled them out of their jobs and their money; while somehow looking them square in the eye every day, with a smile on their faces, sometimes for years at a time.

Who tend to be the biggest violators of values?

Sooner or later, everyone violates their own values to some degree—sometimes consciously, sometimes not—sometimes large, sometimes small. But the most *visible and insidious* violators are, I think, anyone in a position of power who asks for the trust of others then knowingly deceives them. Corrupt politicians, dishonest CEOs and pedophile priests come to mind—and they bring it all on themselves. They are *visible* because they're in the public eye every day, and *insidious* because they have direct impact on a constituency of people to whom they owe impeccable trustworthiness. There are others who are equally as visible—pro athletes, television and movie stars, and other famous people—but they are not "insidious" because they only have *in*direct impact on our lives and there is no "trust deal" between them and us.

But let's look just at politicians for a moment. They have *direct impact* by creating laws or making lifestyle decisions that affect us. So their violations are on a higher plane. They actually asked for our trust to get elected, then threw it back in our faces. Our American political system, beautiful as it is, actually invites the violation of values by politicians. Why? Let's dissect it. A politician only has power by being in office, can only obtain office by getting votes, and can only get votes by convincing a large body of people they have like views. So, connecting the dots, a politician must succumb to the temptation of misrepresenting his own views by telling different things to opposing groups, all in an attempt to win more votes than opponents and obtain office or stay in it. The ultimate "watchdog" of a politician is the media, which broadcasts incongruities on the 11 o'clock news. But make no mistake about it, while our political system may invite it, *it is the behavioral choice of the politician to actually do it.* It's their fault, not the fault of the system.

What's even worse is, when called to task for it, the politician artfully dodges the questions and accusations with endless diatribes of pure baloney—a skill that must be mastered if they hope to serve multiple terms—secure in the knowledge that many people won't see it, and those who do are likely to forgive and forget over time. Case closed, re-election secure.

Politicians who are mistrusted are guilty of a self-inflicted gunshot—because so few of them say what they stand for and then stick to it come hell or high water. Translation: they violate their own values. In other words, those things they may actually believe in the most, they are willing to disavow if it means garnering more votes. Said in another way: a politician's "greater good" is not to serve the public, which it should be, but to do what must be done to obtain and stay in office. Shakespeare said everyone has a "tragic flaw." I believe a democratic political system is the best on earth; but this is the tragic flaw in such a system.

Having said all that, I'm delighted to point out that some politicians will not succumb to it. Abraham Lincoln put his re-election on the line by staying true to what he believed was his highest presidential obligation—preserving the union—which caused him to stay the course of the war in the face of overwhelming opposition. As the election approached, the North was losing the Civil War, he was ridiculed and second-guessed daily in newspapers, had lost the support of many in his own party, and faced the tide of public opinion that was going against him. He could have caved in to all of it, changed his mind on a variety of issues, and preserved his re-election. He didn't. He stood on principal, virtually alone. And only a last-minute reversal in the war and ultimate Union victory turned him into a hero who won re-election. But let's not miss the ultimate point of this story: the fickle masses were willing to change their values, and one gutsy guy wasn't.

Another example: Peter Ueberroth ran for California governor in 2004 and made a high-integrity decision to stay true to his values—that most would not have. With a month to go before election, he was so far behind in the polls because of being a virtual unknown to younger and ethnic voters, that the only way he could close the gap in that short a time was to engage in negative mud-slinging and bringing his opponents down. How often do we see that tactic employed? Frankly, we see it in just about every election. But we didn't see it with Ueberroth. Faced with that choice, he surprised everyone by dropping out of the race, refusing to abandon his positive campaign. His desire to be governor wasn't less than the others. He just made a conscious and courageous decision to remain true to his values—to win on his own merits, to not degrade others, or not run at all. How many politicians would have made that same decision? Too darn few.

As a result, the closer it gets to election day, the more ugly and nasty it gets. The value of human dignity is tossed out the window. That's tragic.

That's also why I decided long ago I would never seek public office. By sticking to a high-road, positive-only campaign—my only approach—I don't believe it's possible to win. I would state my opinions and positions on the issues, and not budge, thereby alienating those who felt differently, and never getting their votes. Being wishy-washy gets you elected. Being firm in your beliefs is another matter.

How to tell when someone is violating her own values.

It's pretty simple: what she *does* doesn't match what she *says*. That's an integrity outage and a sign of value violation. Here's the formula: Our *values* drive our *decisions*, which drive our *behaviors*. Said in reverse: each behavior is the result of a decision, which is built from a value. So guess what is the single-best clue to a person's values. Their behaviors. Regardless of what they *say* they value, their actions speak louder, and that's what people will watch and emulate. Words are cheap; actions paint the truer picture.

Parents who smoke and forbid their kids to do it because they say it causes cancer—who do they think they're fooling? The kids may "get it" that health is at risk, but they'll still think it's okay to smoke *because their parents do it*. Take a person who is dead-set against drug use, but who just "goes long" because everyone else is doing it and doesn't want to be laughed at as the outcast. Caving in is not an option if you are truly committed to your values.

Most people are more concerned with making friends and not making enemies than with remaining true to their values; and as such, will violate their own values at the virtual drop of a hat. Here's a key point: *it can be painful to live your values every day*. Because it forces you to make choices that are uncomfortable, like dealing with people whose values clash with yours. Those people could be a best friend, a next-door neighbor, a co-worker, a family member, or even a spouse. There's a price for living your values, and most aren't willing to pay it. Sometimes that price means a frank conversation about your opposing beliefs and other times it may mean letting go of the relationship altogether because it's undermining your mental health. Here's a huge clue: if you know someone whose behavior is unacceptable to you and who drives you nuts, you two have a values clash. Remaining an active partner in that relationship will wear you down. Even worse, you may, over time, begin to forgive the behavior and ultimately adopt it yourself, perhaps without even knowing it. Is that what you want? If not, then you have to deal with it and stop ignoring it. That's what I mean by uncomfortable. Take action.

Strong, confident, and self-assured people are less concerned that others agree with them and more committed to being true to themselves. And here's the best news: if that's not you—if you feel you're too weak to stand on your principals—then deciding to live your values, and then actually *living them* on an everyday basis, will *build* that strength, confidence, and self-assuredness. You'll soon possess the same qualities you've long admired in others and become the person you've always wanted.

Why care about living your values? What are the benefits of doing so and the penalties if you don't?

Our values provide us the ability to do two critical things: make smarter decisions and build more productive people relationships.

That said, the benefits of living your values are many, such as:

- Making more intelligent decisions, in the moment, that will keep you inside your value system and not take you "out of bounds,"
- Making many more decisions either black or white, with far fewer lodged in the gray,
- Making better "people selections" in your life, including picking truer friends and letting go of negative, unproductive relationships,
- Being a leader with high integrity who does what she says,
- Being more consistent on value-based decisions, not wishy-washy, and therefore building a more loyal following, whether you're a parent, a coach, a CEO, a manager, a teacher, or whoever.

Is anything in that list *un*attractive to you?

On the flip side, the penalties of not living your values are also many such as:

- Losing friends,
- Alienating family,
- Fewer job opportunities,
- Losing sales,
- Losing customers,

- Getting fired from jobs
- Terminating marriages and business partnerships—two of the most financially and emotionally devastating events in anyone's life.

Any or all of the above can take a toll on your health. How many of these do you want on *your* plate? If there were a way to rid your life of those havoc-wreaking penalties, would you be interested? Hang in there with me, that's where we're headed next.

Let's paint a clear portrait of values.

Picture a pro football field: 100 yards long and 53+ yards wide with thick white lines down both sides. When a ball carrier, headed for the end zone, steps on or over a sideline, what happens next? No mystery—a referee's whistle blows, the play is dead, the ball is returned to the center of the field, and play resumes.

Let's be more specific about what just happened, however. The ball carrier broke a firm, written rule that defines the acceptable limits of fair, in-bounds play, clearly marked by the thick white lines on the sides. Conclusion: when a rule is broken, everything comes to a halt. The "rules cops"—the referees—assess the violation, determine and take corrective action. It's a simple procedure to follow because it's all written down right there in the rule book; both teams have one, everyone has read and memorized it, and most decisions by the referees go unchallenged because of it.

Now shift away from a football game, to real life. Let's say you're having lunch with a male business client who points across the restaurant to an attractive woman drinking alone at the bar. Your client suggests that you go strike up a conversation with her, invite her to join your table and introduce her to him. You squirm in your chair and look unsettled. He notices your uneasiness and makes a subtle remark about how his company's review committee is considering other providers for the same service now bought from you. Okay, now it's clear: he's pressuring you into getting that woman for him or else risk losing the account. It's decision point for you. You have very little time. He's waiting; the clock is ticking. What do you do?

Think that's a crazier-than-truth example? Actually it happens every day. But it doesn't matter—you pick any scenario in which you are offered two choices, both of which put you deep in the discomfort zone with very little decision time—what do you do?

Here's my point. Wouldn't it be nifty if, just at the point of making one of those difficult life decisions, you had, standing next to you with a look of fierce determination in his eye, a referee with a whistle in his mouth and your personal life rule book in his hip pocket, ready to blow that whistle like an air raid siren if you make the wrong choice? Well the truth is, in real life, that referee just ain't there. You're on your own, sport. To make the right decision, you had better have three things: (1) your written personal life rulebook, (2) that rulebook memorized, and (3) the unyielding courage to stay within your rules, despite all temptation, despite the penalties, despite the risks.

What should be in your rulebook? Your core values—the deeply-felt, hard-and-fast nonnegotiable, behavioral boundaries of your life that are equivalent to thick while lines, left and right, clearly defining the outer edges of your acceptable field of play—your value system, decided upon by you and you alone.

When you have your core values on paper, written with crystal clarity and memorized fully, you have the most potent set of decision-making criteria you'll ever need, any time, anywhere, for any situation. Stick to them with religious zeal and you'll never make a tough decision again that's "out of bounds" for you. Wow! That's an indescribable feeling of personal power.

The basics: how to determine, identify and clarify your own values.

The good news: you already have a set of values, so identifying them is a process of discovery, not creation. But if they're fuzzy and unclear, they can lead to shaky, regret-filled decisions, and this may already have happened to you. So let's bring them out of the fog and into the bright sunshine. Here's how:

Complete the following four questions with specific *behaviors.* Anything less than brutal honesty is a waste of time. Be deadly serious.

- *I feel fire-breathing anger toward other people when they.....*(do what?)
- *I feel great about—and drawn to—other people when they.....*(do what?)
- *I feel ashamed, disgusted or angry with myself when I.....*(do what?)
- *I feel fabulous about—and proud of—myself when I.....*(do what?)

Write in as many behaviors as you can think of for each question. For the first question your answers should describe incredibly maddening, disgusting, and infuriating behaviors that make you want to disengage from the person. For the second question, describe behaviors that create for you a strong attraction, a bond, a rapport and magnetic draw to that person. Be just as passionate with the third and fourth questions that are about you.

Your answers will not *be* your values, but rather *clues* to your values. When you believe you've captured as many as there are, you're ready to craft them into value statements, each one being short (probably one sentence) and clearly and fully defining the limit of your belief on that point. (Note: "Belief" is synonymous with value, as are "philosophy," "code of conduct," "standard of behavior," "personal ethics," and so on. Don't be confused—they're all values.)

I do not believe in one-word or short-phrase values. They're simply not long enough to adequately define a clear boundary. Nor do I believe in paragraph-long or page-long values. They're not short enough to be memorized. Keep it to about a sentence—even a long one—but not much more.

Below are some examples of my values, written as I have them memorized. (Forgive the male pronoun throughout, which I use generically. Don't over interpret; it just means I'm a guy, not sexist.)

I believe that every individual must accept personal responsibility for his thoughts, choices and actions and not blame other people or circumstances for his misfortunes.

I believe there is no failure—only undesirable outcomes from which we learn, grow and improve.

I believe that life comes with no securities, no guarantees and no entitlements, that it is highly unpredictable, uncertain and unfair, and that each person must accept his own responsibility and seize his own opportunities to survive and thrive in that environment.

I believe in winning—in the energy it creates, the teamwork it requires, and most importantly, in the exhilarating thrill of self-worth it provides.

I believe that enthusiastic self-confidence is the single most important quality in a human being, upon which all others are based, and that it is the foundation for all high-performance achievement. I also believe the best guarantee of a successful conclusion to a doubtful undertaking is a person's devout belief in the beginning that he can do it.

I have more, but you get the idea. Please don't misunderstand my purpose in sharing these; I am in no way intending to push you into accepting my beliefs. I merely wish to show you a writing format you may choose to model. That said, however, if any values match yours, take them word for word, or modify them to fit you. Values are not proprietary.

Once committed to paper, read them every single day, word for word, for as many weeks, months or years as it takes to fully commit them to memory. Remember, when you're faced with a tough decision, you don't want to call in a search team to find your values. If they are memorized, decisions over which you used to vacillate can be made almost instantaneously. You'll reach a point where you don't even need to think about your values when deciding; you'll just instinctively know what's right.

One last idea: since you're human and fully capable of making dumb mistakes—like making a decision outside your value system even when you're clear on your values—you might consider appointing "values cops" in your life to hold you accountable. Remember, even an under-par golfer can't see his own back swing and needs a coach to point out the flaws. I suggest you identify trustworthy, caring, like-minded, success-driven people in your life who want the best for you with no ulterior motive— and anoint them to be your whistleblowers. I have chosen a small group of people who know me best: my wife, my adult twin children, and a group of fellow CEOs whom I meet with monthly. With them on my side, I am well served. Who will be your "values cops"?

With all this, you just created the football field analogy in our own life. Nice going.

You're off and running on a high-integrity life.

Remember: memorize, memorize, memorize your values so you don't have to find them when a "moment of truth" arrives. Use the above process to discover your own values, then commit to living them every day, with every decision you make and every action you take.

You'll be the person everyone wants to call his "trusted friend." Is there a higher compliment?

About The Author

Rick Houcek

Rick Houcek's singular company purpose is: To provide high-octane, world-class strategic planning systems for business and life, helping Top Gun leaders, teams and individuals to succeed "on purpose, most of the time," rather than "by accident, some of the time." He does this four primary ways: (1) facilitating his Power Planning™ strategic planning retreats for small and mid-size companies, (2) leading his Passion Planning™ workshops for ambitious individuals on personal life planning and goal setting, (3) delivering high-energy motivational keynotes, and (4) one-on-one success coaching. He has coached entrepreneurs, CEOs, presidents, and senior executives for over 10 years, and is former president of Ross Roy Advertising, an Atlanta ad agency and division of the $700 million Ross Roy Group. A University of Missouri graduate, he is a member of the National Speakers Association and has been recognized in Who's Who Among U.S. Executives and Who's Who in Georgia. Rick is married and passionately devoted to his soul mate, adores his awesome grown twins, and has four fanatical life passions: his family, his personal health and fitness, helping others prosper through his business and friendships, and playing competitive baseball on a traveling men's team.

Rick Houcek, President
Soar With Eagles, Inc.
5398 Hallford Drive
Atlanta, Georgia 30338
Phone: 770-391-9122
Fax: 770-393-0076
Email: Rick@SoarWithEagles.com
www.SoarWithEagles.com